Hey Dad, It's Me!

Hey Dad, It's Me!

Discover the Father
Who *Loves* and *Protects* You

Julie McGhghy

Hey Dad, It's Me! Discover the Father Who Loves and Protects You
© Copyright 2021 Julie McGhghy

All rights reserved. No part of this publication may be reproduced, distributed or transmitted in any form or by any means, including photocopying, recording, or other electronic or mechanical methods, without the prior written permission of Julie McGhghy (the author), except in the case of brief quotations embodied in critical reviews and certain other noncommercial uses permitted by copyright law.

Although the author has made every effort to ensure that the information in this book was correct at press time, the author and Confidence Publishing (the publisher) do not assume and hereby disclaim any liability to any party for any loss, damage, or disruption caused by errors or omissions, whether such errors or omissions result from negligence, accident, or any other cause.

Neither the author nor the publisher assumes any responsibility or liability whatsoever on behalf of the consumer or reader of this material. Any perceived slight of any individual or organization is purely unintentional.

Scripture verses quoted are from the King James Version (KJV) unless otherwise identified. Scripture verses marked (AMP) are from the AMPLIFIED BIBLE, Copyright © 1954, 1958, 1962, 1964, 1965, 1987 by The Lockman Foundation. Scripture verses from the KJV and the AMP are from the King James Version / Amplified Bible Parallel Edition, Copyright © 1995 by The Zondervan Corporation. Scripture verses marked (NIV) are from the Holy Bible, New International Version®, NIV® Copyright ©1973, 1978, 1984, 2011 by Biblica, Inc.®. Used by permission. All rights reserved.

For more information, email julie@confidenceingod.com.
Published in West Chester, Ohio.

Library of Congress Cataloging-in-Publication Data
Name: McGhghy, Julie, author.
Title: Hey Dad, It's Me! Discover the Father Who Loves and Protects You
Description: West Chester, Ohio: Confidence Publishing [2021]
Identifiers: Library of Congress Control Number: 2021917504 / ISBN 978-1-7377361-0-3 /ISBN 978-1-7377361-1-0 (Ebook) / ISBN 978-1-7377361-2-7 (alk. Paper) / ISBN 978-1-7377361-3-4 (Audiobook) / ISBN 978-1-7377361-4-1 (Spanish) / ISBN 978-1-7377361-5-8 (Spanish: ebook) / ISBN 978-1-7377361-6-5 (Spanish: alk. paper) / ISBN 978-1-7377361-7-2 (Spanish: Audiobook)

LC record available at https://lccn.loc.gov/2021917504

GET YOUR FREE RESOURCE!

Throughout this book I share how God has fathered me and encourage you to prayerfully consider how He has been there for you also.

If you sometimes find you lack confidence that God wants to hear your prayers or that He listens and will answer your prayers, I invite you to access this free resource I created for you.

Readers who download and read *How to Have Confidence in Your Prayer Life* will be encouraged to learn God does not expect perfect prayers, we can come to Him in our brokenness, and He will grant us wisdom and understanding.

You will also find a number of biblical examples of prayer that may assist you as you seek to find God's fatherly hand in your life.

You can get a copy by visiting:
http://confidenceingod.com/heydad/

Dedications

To my husband, who walked with me through all kinds of crazy while pointing me to my heavenly Father. And who has been a wonderful father to our three children and an amazing grandfather to our eight grandkids.

Your undying love and support gave me strength to walk back through my life and find God at every step, even the difficult ones.

You're still the best!

To Reverend Norman R. Paslay II, what a difference you made in my life!

Your dedication to your family was a beautiful example for me. And your commitment to teaching others how to live according to God's established structure for the family empowered me to look back on my shattered upbringing and find God at every turn.

Thank you for teaching me to listen to the voice of God and encouraging me to write this book.

Foreward

In your hands you hold a book that I believe addresses one of the deepest, most common needs in the Church today. Paul wrote to the Corinthians that *"they had not many fathers"*. Things have not changed for God's people in the centuries that have passed since those words were written by the great apostle. While Paul's words had a spiritual context at the time he wrote, this phrase encapsulates the sad reality of our world, even within the Church.

While I personally was blessed with an amazing earthly father, I realized at a young age that not everyone was as blessed as I. Sadly, for many the concept of God as a Heavenly Father brings mixed emotions. For some the idea is unrelatable or even undesirable. This is because their natural father has been absent in some measure or a devastating disappointment.

How can those who hurt in this way reconcile the pain of their reality with the promise of a Heavenly Father who loves them unconditionally? This book will help you find the answers in the most reliable source, the Word of God. Through Julie's *letters to her father* she will openly address the many ways God has filled that void in her own life. She does this masterfully not only through her testimony, but by directing us to the *love letter written to all of us by God our Father*.

David wrote in Psalms 27:10, "when my father and my mother forsake me then the Lord will take me up". This is Julie's testimony, and it can be yours too. Whatever your earthly father has been or not been, I believe this book can help you confront the past and pursue God's future for you. May we all have a personal revelation of God's deep love for us and identify with Him as our own "Abba, Father."

Rev. Kristen Ellis, Pastor, The Calvary Church Cincinnati, Ohio

Table of Contents

Introduction: 1
A Surreal Encounter

1 Reaching Out: 5
Introducing My Heavenly Father

2 Inherited Characteristics: 15
We Will Be Like Him

3 Unconditional Love: 33
He Loves You with an Everlasting Love

4 Religion Versus Christianity: 43
How We Live the Difference

5 Authority Figure: 59
He Is the Source of Our Support and Guidance

6 Boundaries: 73
God's Loving Source of Security

7 Beyond the Boundaries: 85
God's Protection

8 A Place of Safety: 105
God is a Refuge

9 By the Numbers: 121
We are More Than a Statistic

10 Self-Image: 139
What Do You See in the Mirror?

11 Acceptance: 153
We Do Not Need to Struggle to Be Part of the Family

12 Identity: 167
He Gives You a Name

13 God's Transforming Love: 177
Turning Regrets into Thanksgiving

Introduction:

A Surreal Encounter

The encounter was surreal! At the age of sixteen, I found myself talking to my biological father for the first time. My father had divorced my mom when I was a toddler, and he had let her second husband adopt me when I was five years old. He had called that day and asked me to meet him at a nearby Denny's. I didn't know what else to say except, "Sure, I'll be there in thirty minutes." I grabbed my purse, told my mom where I was going and drove to Denny's to meet my father.

I had never seen a picture of him, so I had no idea how to identify my dad. I was a bit dazed, not knowing what to think or how to feel. I parked my car, got out, and hung around on the sidewalk outside Denny's waiting for some man to come introduce himself to me. Instead, a woman I didn't know walked up and asked, "Are you Julie?" She told me my dad was waiting inside.

We didn't eat at Denny's but rather went to my maternal grandmother's home where we could visit. I don't remember much of what was said. I am not even certain my dad and I talked much at all. It seemed more like a reunion of my dad and my grandmother. On the surface it appeared to be nothing more than an evening visiting a new acquaintance. My father hugged me when I dropped him off at Denny's two hours later, but the hug didn't feel like love. It felt like an obligation. The entire evening was a bit awkward. This whole experience has always seemed like a dream because I had been asleep when he called me, and I went back to sleep when I returned home.

For the next several years after that meeting, Dad and I developed a long-distance relationship. He invited me to his home in New Hampshire after I graduated from high school. That was when I learned that the woman who talked to me outside of Denny's was his wife. It was also the first time I met the children he had with that wife, the ones that would have been my half-siblings if Dad were still my legal father.

Dad also came to my college graduation, which was several years later since I did not go to college directly after high school. He visited me three times over the years (including that night at Denny's), and I visited him a handful of times. Between those visits we occasionally communicated by email or phone, but it was difficult to develop a close father-daughter relationship. We had so few memories together; thus, we had little to build a relationship on.

At Dad's funeral, I learned another reason why he and I had experienced such a difficult time developing a relationship. He felt guilty about leaving me and my brother, Randy, when we were young and he had divorced our mother. This guilt impaired his ability to develop a close relationship with me.

After learning of his guilt, I mentally constructed letters I would have sent him had I known. I told him all the ways God had fathered me in his absence, assuring him that he didn't need to feel guilty. But I never had an opportunity to write those letters and share them.

Later it occurred to me that these letters could serve a broader purpose: to help other people who have struggled in their relationships with their own fathers see how God loves us and actively fathers us through life, regardless of the missteps or failures of our own earthly fathers. As I have taught and ministered for more than thirty years, I have often encountered people who do not feel loved or lovable because their fathers did not love them. They feel invisible. They resist close, intimate relationships because they view such relationships as only temporary, always ending with much pain. They fear continuing the dysfunctional cycle because they are confident they are just like their fathers.

These people usually transfer these feelings onto God, believing that since their own fathers did not love them, God would not love them either, or even see them. Though they may be able to declare by faith that God is "God the Father" and their "heavenly Father," they are unable to see that God has actively fathered them. They cannot develop a close, intimate relationship with their heavenly Father and dare not dream of truly becoming Christ-like.

I have shared my story with many of those people, and the vast majority have found it helpful. The purpose of this book is to help people who struggle to recognize God's fatherly hand in their lives. My story illustrates God is not just our heavenly Father; He also actively fathers us because He loves us.

As I mentioned before, I don't have many memories of my biological father. Much of what I will discuss in this book came either straight from him, things I pieced together over time in my observations or what people said to me about my father. Some of what I describe in the events, circumstances and characteristics of people and places may not be totally accurate, for human memories are not totally accurate, but they are based on my experiences, observations and recollections over a lifetime.

Each chapter of *Hey Dad, It's Me!* begins with one of my letters to Dad explaining why he does not need to feel guilty about leaving me when I was young. I address some aspect of fathering that God fulfilled in Dad's absence in a much greater way than Dad could have. These are things God has taught me during my adult years as I grew in my faith. The letters are written from my adult perspective and as if I could still send them to Dad, as if he were still alive, because my heart aches that I did not share such things with him before he passed away.

Each letter begins with "Hey Dad, it's me!" because that is how I recall addressing the first Father's Day card I sent to Dad when I was fourteen. I had just learned my maternal grandmother knew how to reach him, so I sent him a Father's Day card to start communicating with him. All I could think to say as an opening was "Hey Dad, it's me!"

Then in each chapter, I share with you more details about my experiences and God's fatherly actions. I support these actions through scriptures that lead you into God's Word and illuminates God's fatherly love for you. I realize you may not be a Christian believer, but I will address you as a Christian. It is my way of showing you respect, treating you as a fellow brother or sister as you discover how God fathered me. If you have not yet entered into a relationship with God through salvation, I pray that as you read this book, you will desire such a relationship and will at any time seek a pastor and church who can guide you into a relationship with Jesus Christ and adoption into the family of God.

Also, as you read this book, I encourage you to reflect upon your own life and experiences and search for God's fatherly hand. I hope you learn that no matter what your relationship with your father has been and how you feel about your father and about yourself, you are not fatherless. God has lovingly fathered you all the days of your life.

1

Reaching Out:

Introducing My Heavenly Father

Hey Dad, it's me!

I know it has been a while since we last talked, which really isn't anything new. For a lot of years, we have touched base every now and then, but certainly not frequently; yet when we touch base, we seem to pick up where we left off before. Nothing has ever really changed through the years. So, I am touching base again, but this time with an intention of changing things. This time I want to share my heart, and maybe we can get to know each other a bit better.

You have been on my mind for a long time, but I haven't been able to contact you. So, I am reaching out to you now in hopes that I will someday see you again. My purpose for writing, in addition to wishing we knew each other better, is to address something someone told me the last time I was in your home. I was told that having a relationship with me was difficult for you because you felt so guilty.

I have thought of that so often since then, and I want you to know that you have nothing to feel guilty about. I suppose if the guilt hadn't been in the way we would know each other better, and you would know that I don't condemn you and am not angry at you for anything you did or didn't do. I was actually a bit shocked when I heard you felt guilty.

I am clearly not a psychologist, but I understand from a cognitive perspective that guilt is an emotion people experience when they are convinced they have caused harm.[1] Generally, there are five causes of guilt: 1) something you did; 2) something you didn't do, but want to; 3) something you think you did; 4) thinking you didn't do enough to help someone; and 5) thinking you are doing better than someone else.[2] It is possible the guilt you have felt stems from all five of these causes, but I want you to know you do not need to feel guilty.

I can understand why you might feel some guilt. I am sure life would have been different had you stayed and provided a stable home for Randy and me. Maybe I would have been able to stay in a single elementary school and junior high school as I grew up instead of going to four different elementary schools and two different junior high schools. I was fortunate to attend only one high school, but that was just because at the time there was only one in town. I can remember living in twelve different places before I graduated from high school. I am certain there were more in my younger years that I just cannot remember.

Maybe if you had stayed, I could have continued the dance lessons that I loved. I don't know how old I was when Mom enrolled me, but I know I had to quit the lessons when I was nine because we moved out of town. I remember Mom searching for a dance school in the new town, but I was never enrolled in one.

There are a lot of maybes I could mention but won't because I don't care to focus on the what-could-have-beens. As it was, I bounced between poverty and living in nice neighborhoods, depending on Mom's marital status at the time. I didn't live at any one location long enough to develop close, lasting friendships.

I am sure life would have been different had you been there to raise Randy and me, but I don't know if it would have been better or worse. Maybe I would have had better self-esteem, which would have made me more confident and able to make better decisions as I got older. Maybe I would have known how to stay out of situations with boys and men that I didn't know how to handle at the time. Maybe I wouldn't have married at eighteen. But, Dad, I don't want the what-could-have-beens to be the basis for our relationship. I don't want to focus on them because I am confident that God was with me through it all.

You are my father. Notwithstanding, you gave up that legal right when I was about five. In my heart, however, you will always be my father. But in your absence during most of my life, God fathered me in a way you never could have. He loved me with an unconditional, everlasting love that no natural father can offer. He watched over me and guarded me more consistently than any natural father could. And when things were hard, when life seemed unfair, He worked things out for my good. No natural father can do these things. And you could not have done them either.

In future letters to you I hope to explain more fully why you do not need to feel guilty. I am the person God intended for me to be at this point. He continues molding me into the person He wants me to grow into.

Well, I suppose I've shared enough for this first contact. I will reach out again soon.

From me, the one who always wanted to be "your little girl!"

Julie

A Bit of the Background

Welcome. Thank you for joining me on this journey through my memories, observations and realizations of how I have been fathered throughout my life, even though I didn't have a consistent father figure in my life. This realization didn't happen overnight, and some parts of it may not make a lot of sense to you. Yet I am confident it is true.

As I shared in the letter to Dad at the beginning of this chapter, the reason I started reflecting on my life and my father was a comment made to me by someone close to him explaining that Dad had felt guilty about not being in my life as I grew up. This caused him the inability to develop a close father/daughter relationship with me once we met when I was sixteen. That was a shock to me. I never considered that he would feel guilty. From my perspective, life is just life. Some things happen, and some things don't. But there is a purpose for each of our lives, and God works it all out for good when we love Him and strive to find and accomplish His purpose in our lives.[3]

Please don't get the idea that my life was perfect. It was not. Some might say it was far from perfect, and there were things that are hard to view through the eyes of faith in a loving God. But, as Ben Cerullo writes, "When you see things through the eyes of faith, God always is bigger than your problems. Fear, anxiety, and hopelessness melt away in the light of His glory."[4] As I began reflecting on my life, I realized I was not actively fathered by any of the four men my mother married and divorced during my childhood; yet I was not fatherless.

God Actively Fathers Us

We all have a heavenly Father who loves us.[5] As Christians, we know Jesus is our everlasting Father.[6] Yet we often accept "everlasting Father" as one of Jesus's titles without recognizing that He actively fathers us. In the next few paragraphs, I will share just a few examples of how Jesus has fathered me, which I will expound on in the following chapters.

We usually look at parents as role models in our lives. They teach us how to behave in society and in our own homes when we reach adulthood. If they haven't loved and protected us as we needed during childhood, we tend to fear we will be just like them when we are adults. But we don't have to be just like them. In fact, our heavenly Father through the Holy Spirit makes us Christ-like: "But we all, with open face beholding as in a glass the glory of the Lord, are changed into the same image from glory to glory, *even* as by the Spirit of the Lord."[7] God fathers us by forming us in His image and helping us to mature to be Christ-like. When we do not feel our parents' love, perhaps viewing them as lacking patience and gentleness toward us, we do not need to fear that we will also be impatient and harsh. As we reflect on our lives, we will see that God helped us mature in the fruit of the Spirit which is "love, joy, peace, longsuffering, gentleness, goodness, faith, meekness, temperance."[8] One way God fathers us is by helping us become responsible, loving, mature adults.

God also fathers us by loving us unconditionally. When our parents aren't consistent in their love for us, we begin feeling unloved. We may even wonder if God can possibly love us if our own parents didn't fulfill that basic role of a parent. When God told Jeremiah, "I have loved thee with an everlasting love,"[9] He did not mean this for Jeremiah's ears only. God loves us (you and me) with an everlasting, unconditional love. *There is nothing we can do to end His love for us.* He lavishes on us His great love, calling us children of God.[10] How do we know? Because when sin entered into the world through Adam and Eve and separated us from God,[11] He came into the world and died in our place so that our relationship with Him may be restored.[12] Even today when we mess up, when we miss the mark, God continues to love us. There is nothing we can do to fall outside of God's love.

And for my last example, please consider how we all long to be part of a healthy, functional family. When we have been raised in dysfunction with absent fathers, whether physically or emotionally absent, we dream of being part of a cohesive family. And that is exactly what God provides us when we become part of the family of God.

God creates a healthy, loving family among His children.[13] We have Christian brothers and sisters to walk through life with us. We are taught to be good to one another[14] and to rejoice with each other when one of us is honored.[15] When one of our brothers or sisters suffer, we all suffer together.[16] Jesus Himself was an example of love for us and taught us to love one another as He loved us.[17]

In this family we are given elders who guide us like grandparents, parents, aunts, and uncles would in a healthy, natural family. We are instructed not to rebuke our elders but to show them respect by encouraging them as we would our fathers and mothers.[18] And the elders are to teach the younger generations how to live and conduct themselves.[19] We are set in the family of God with everything we need to live in love, functioning like the healthy family we have all dreamed of. This family gathers together and encourages one another.[20]

The family of God is not perfect; after all, it is comprised of human beings. We have sibling rivalry. Often siblings fight and complain because each one feels their parents treat other siblings better, such as spending more time with them or buying nicer things for them. Similarly, Christian brothers and sisters may get disgruntled because they feel the pastor or music director gives other people more opportunity to minister, such as speaking in church services or singing specials more often. We have the younger testing the boundaries of the older. The older brothers and sisters still like singing hymns while the younger ones prefer upbeat praise songs, and they will push the boundaries of the traditional songs. But God gives instructions for handling such things in a loving, healthy manner. We are to be merciful, kind, humble, meek, patient, forgiving.[21] God gives us a family of God that is loving, functional and fulfills all that we have dreamed of for a family. He is our Father; thus, we are not fatherless at all!

Contemplate How God Fathers You

In this book I will share with you many events and circumstances from my life and how God fathered me through them all. I am not, and you are not, fatherless, no matter what our relationships with our earthly fathers look like. You are not fatherless even if you have never met your earthly father. As you read this book and see how God fathered me, think on your own life and consider the areas in which your father seems to have fallen short. Consider how God helped you overcome those things. Reflect on your own life and see anew how God has fathered you.

Write these things down for further prayerful contemplation. Let God show you how He has fathered you as you read the next chapter about the characteristics we inherit.

2

Inherited Characteristics:

We Will Be Like Him

Hey Dad, it's me!

Well, since my last letter I have been contemplating which of your characteristics I inherited at birth. The most obvious of these characteristics are the physical ones.

I found a copy of a picture of you and Mom when you got married. My eyes are the color of Mom's, but I think they are shaped like yours. I have your height, which I thought was a bad thing when I was a teenager because I was taller than all the boys. And I have big feet, which I believe comes from you because of your height.

More important to me are the nonphysical characteristics I inherited from you and Mom. Do you remember when I visited you when I was twenty-two? I doubt I ever shared why I visited you then. Why would a young woman who was obviously pregnant travel by car from Kansas to New Hampshire, along with a two-year-old, to see her father for only the third time in her life?

If I remember correctly, I was about six months pregnant. The doctor told me I could make the trip with my husband if I stopped every hour to stretch my legs. Mike and I packed up our daughter and set out to see you. We took three days to get there and three days to get home. We only stayed with you for three days. What was so important that I would travel that far for only a three-day visit? It was because of these nonphysical characteristics!

As you know, Mom has always battled with mental and emotional issues. I am pretty confident such issues contributed to why you and she divorced. Don't get me wrong, I love Mom and I am convinced she raised us the best she could. But Mom has been hospitalized a number of times during my life. The first time I can remember was when I was thirteen. I have learned from others she had been hospitalized when I was a toddler. Mom was also hospitalized when I was sixteen. And then, when I came to visit you as a twenty-two-year-old, she was hospitalized again.

I didn't always know it at the time, but I have heard from various people that all of these hospitalizations were due to psychiatric issues, and some, if not all, were because she attempted suicide. So, at twenty-two-years old and with my second child on the way, all I could think about was how much like my mother I was. I didn't know you well enough to know what nonphysical characteristics of you I had inherited. The only side of me I knew was my mom. It suddenly became very important to me to get to know you! I had to know that there was another side of me, a steady, responsible, respectable side. I certainly didn't know it at the time, but later in my life that would become even more important to me.

When I visited you, I found you to be . . . stable. How is that for a description? Stable! But stable was important to me. Could it be I had a stable side, one that was not emotionally volatile? You didn't show your emotions much. You were just stable. You didn't overwhelm me with love, but you also didn't reject me or act distracted when I was around. I found great comfort in that. Because you showed so little emotion, I recognized that I too was not very emotional. Both of us seemed to relate to our worlds through facts and experiences--not through emotions. That characteristic has served me well in my home, in my career and in my relationships in general.

In my last letter I mentioned someone had told me that having a relationship with me was difficult because you felt so guilty. I told you that in your absence during most of my life, God fathered me in a way you never could have. That includes the characteristics that I have developed throughout my life. Yes, from you I inherited the shape of my eyes, my height, and my big feet. Even though you weren't present in my life to help build my character, God has been my constant companion. He has never left me, and through the years, the fruit of His Spirit has grown in my life: love, joy, peace, patience, gentleness, goodness, faith, meekness, and self-control. He has made me a loving, happy, patient, care-free person who loves to laugh and have fun! I have even ceased being afraid to show emotions. It is through emotions that I worship Him the deepest.

Although my home life was not stable as I grew up, God let me see in you the stable side of my personality that helped me when things with Mom got difficult. God gave me a husband who has provided our children and me the stability and security we always needed. God has surrounded me with love in many different friendships and spiritual leaders in my life. He went beyond anything you could have done for me. There is no reason for you to feel guilty! God exceeded everything you could have done for me!

Yes, I inherited your eyes. But, more importantly, I want to have my heavenly Father's eyes. Gary Winthur Chapman expressed that best when he wrote "Father's Eyes," performed by Amy Grant.[1] In the song a girl muses about how her mother and the rest of the world views her but expresses her one prayer—that when people look at her life, they will say she has her Father's eyes. Those eyes found the good in things, found the source of help and were full of compassion.

The girl then turns her thoughts to the day when she will stand before the Lord, and she will pay for all the good and bad deeds she has done. Again, she hopes people will stand and say that she's had her Father's eyes.

This song describes the eyes of my heavenly Father. His eyes always found the good in me and in His eyes, I always found help. He was and is my constant source of help. You might remember when I was going through a divorce at the age of nineteen. I called you for help because I was in California, alone, with no transportation. You helped me by co-signing a loan for a car. I was so thankful for that financial help. Yet God was the One who provided emotional help. I was able to run to Him, expressing my shame and fear, and He comforted me with His Word. He told me not to be afraid because He was with me and would strengthen me, help me and hold me by His hand.[2] He also assured me He would instruct me and guide me in the way I should go because He would guide me with His eye.[3]

Dad, I am thankful for your emotional stability that I inherited. And I am thankful God has been with me for emotional support and to guide me through life's difficult paths. He instilled in me eyes full of compassion and a source of help. God comforted me with His Word and guided me with His eye. There is no reason for you to feel guilty. I have my Father's eyes.

From me, the one who always wanted to be "your little girl!"

Julie McGhghy

Longing to Know Who We Are

I have known many teenagers and young adults who have a parent who has not been active in their lives since before they can remember. At the very least these individuals tend to wonder what their biological parents were like. For some of us, the desire to know about our biological parents goes beyond a mild curiosity. Many made-for-TV movies and TV shows have included a character who was adopted or never knew at least one of their biological parents. In these movies and TV shows, the characters either raise the issue in a sensitive discussion with a parent or a family member who has been active in their lives or they initiate an in-depth investigation to find the biological parent.

As an example, I remember Episode 10 of Season 1 of *The Facts of Life* that was titled "Adoption" and first aired on April 25, 1980.[4] When a school project required making a family tree, Natalie refused to complete the project and got visibly upset about the topic. Eventually, she informed her classmates that she was adopted. The ever-nosey, well-connected Blair offers to initiate a search to find Natalie's birth parents. As the search began, Mrs. Garrett attempted reasoning with Natalie about having a real mother and father who chose her as their very own. Natalie declared, "I'm incomplete" after explaining she has an empty space inside because she knows nothing about her biological parents.[5] Ultimately, Mrs. Garrett's reasoning was effective, and Natalie called off the search despite her natural longing to know who her biological parents were.

I have seen this situation play out as a parent myself with a daughter who was adopted by my husband and who had never met her biological father. Trisha's curiosity about her father began when she was sixteen. Just like the people in the made-for-TV movies, Natalie in *The Facts of Life* episode, and me when I was twenty-two, Trisha wanted to know what her other biological parent was like.

21

Hey Dad, It's Me!

Trisha had a good relationship with her dad, the man who adopted her, loved her, raised her as his own, and whom she loves dearly. Yet she wanted to know what her natural father was like. She and I discussed the matter; and for various reasons, including how it would complicate her life, we agreed it wasn't a good idea to search for him at that time; yet that desire to find her father never left her. She continued sporadically searching for him for twenty-plus years.

Not long ago, Trisha found her biological father's obituary on the Internet. After confirming with me that the obituary was in fact for her biological father, she contacted his sister and his surviving spouse. That curiosity, or need to know about her father, never left her despite the fact that she loved and appreciated her dad very much. Even after learning of her biological father's death, she wanted to learn about him from his family. They were kind and gracious when she contacted them. Trisha now has a developing relationship with her biological father's other children and family members. There is just something within us that needs to know what we are made of, and we need to know both of our biological parents, when possible, to satisfy that curiosity, that need, that void.

Most people who do not know their biological father have an inherent need, or at least a desire, to know the other part of themselves that makes up who they are. Many of us who never get the privilege of meeting our biological fathers struggle with insecurities about who we are.

When my mother was hospitalized when I was twenty-two, it overwhelmed me. I spiraled into an identity crisis like I had never before or since experienced. Was I destined to become just like my mother? I loved and cared for my mother, but I did not want to be like my mother to the degree that she had struggled for years with mental and emotional health issues.[6] I didn't just have a curiosity about my father's personality and character. I needed to know who he was as an individual. I needed to know there was part of me that was not mentally and emotionally unstable. When I spent some time with him, I found the stability of character and personality I needed to know were a part of who I am, which held me steady until I matured in Christ and learned that my identity does not depend on who my parents are.

Becoming Christ-Like

Christians are called to be Christ-like. Paul, John and Peter all taught the early Christians to be like Christ.[7] I think Paul said it best in his letter to the church in Ephesus: "Be ye therefore followers of God, as dear children: And walk in love, as Christ also hath loved us, and hath given himself for us an offering and a sacrifice to God for a sweetsmelling savour."[8] But more importantly, Christ Himself taught His disciples to be like Him.[9]

It is important to realize that the call to be Christ-like is a call to be like our heavenly Father. When prophesying about the Messiah (Jesus Christ), Isaiah said His name would be called, among other things, "the mighty God, the everlasting Father."[10] Jesus told Philip, "He that hath seen me hath seen the Father."[11] Christ was the image of the invisible God,[12] and in Him is the fullness of God.[13] Therefore, as we become Christ-like, we become like our heavenly Father.

How do we become like our heavenly Father? First, by God's working all things together for our good. Many Christians know Romans 8:28: "And we know that all things work together for good to them that love God, to them who are the called according to *his* purpose." By reading on to verse 29, we learn that through God's working things out for our good we are conformed to the image of Christ, we become Christ-like.[14] Also, God gives us all things we need in order to be like Him.[15] Like our natural fathers, He provides an example for us, teaches us, and as we mature in Him, the fruit of the Spirit grows in us.

We are children of God by adoption;[16] thus, the characteristics of God are not inherited at birth. Just as young children who are adopted become like their parents in the years they are under their parents' care, we also become like our heavenly Father as we grow under God's care. The adoptive earthly parents serve as examples for their adopted children. In contrast, God gave us Jesus Christ as our example.

Jesus explained to His disciples that they are to mimic His example. After the mother of James and John asked Jesus to grant her sons the seats on His right and left in His kingdom, Jesus explained to His disciples that just as He came to serve, so shall those who wish to be great serve.[17] Also, after washing His disciples' feet, He made it clear that He did so as an example for them.[18] Since emulating His example was so important, He commanded His disciples to love one another as He loved them.[19]

The apostles understood that they and all Christians are to be like Christ and mirror His example. When the church was being persecuted, the apostle Peter encouraged the Christians to follow Jesus's steps and bear up under the persecution, refraining from speaking falsely or hatefully in return, refraining from sin and trusting God.[20] The apostle John reminded Christians that they should walk as Christ walked.[21] He also helped Christians identify what love is by pointing to Jesus's example.[22]

Even the apostle Paul, who was not an eyewitness to Jesus's life, understood Christians are to live, as well as to lead, by Christ's example, as he demonstrated when he said, "Be ye followers of me, even as I also *am* of Christ."[23] He also encouraged the church to walk in love and forgive just as Christ did.[24]

God provides us all we need to be like Him, our heavenly Father, regardless of who our natural parents are, their inherent traits and their behavior. Giving us Jesus as an example is just one part of what He provides for us. He also teaches us to be like Him.

God teaches us in many ways, just as our natural parents do.[25] Like our natural parents teach us by giving us instruction and correcting us when we are wrong, God teaches us through His Word.[26] By learning through God's

Word, we mature in Him and become like Him.[27] The writer of Hebrews explains we respect our natural parents when they correct us, yet they do so only as they consider proper and good.[28] On the other hand, God's correction is certainly for our good, to make us like Him.[29] God also corrects us because He loves us.[30]

I can remember the first time I heard someone quote James 1:22, "But be ye doers of the word, and not hearers only, deceiving your own selves." Have you ever sat in church, listened to the sermon, and thought to yourself, *Wow, the preacher is really speaking to so-and-so today*? I must confess I have been guilty of that a time or two. And the "so-and-so" was usually one of my children or my husband. Then I heard someone else quote James 1:22. I was reminded to be a doer, not a hearer only. That means I should be listening to the sermon and applying it to my life, not someone else's life. If all I do is listen and not apply the truth to my life, then I deceive myself, and must be corrected by the Word.

As we draw closer to God and wish to understand more, all we need to do is ask Him. The apostle James understood we can ask God for wisdom, and He will give it to us liberally, without reproaching us or making us feel bad for asking.[31] I fondly recall an example of asking God for understanding and receiving it from Him. My husband and I were training to ride our bicycles for a two hundred-mile, two-day fundraising event. We were preparing to ride one hundred miles on two consecutive days.

Preparing to bike long distances includes building one's muscles, cardiovascular system and backside. Sitting on a bicycle saddle for five to seven hours is not comfortable and makes it necessary to condition one's rear end to build endurance. My husband and I trained by riding our bikes twenty miles three nights each week, and then we rode longer distances on Saturdays to build up to a hundred miles.

The first year we rode in the fundraiser, we trained at the Little Miami Scenic River Trail, an abandoned railroad track that had been converted to a paved trail by the Rails-to-Trails Conservancy. The trail runs fifty miles along the Little Miami River through forests and valleys, affording many opportunities to observe—hopefully not too closely—the wildlife in the area. The next year we branched off onto country roads, which again afforded opportunities to observe wildlife.

As I spent so many hours in nature, I learned to really appreciate God's creation. I would also pray while on my bike. God seemed to increasingly show me different animals as I rode, which always delighted me. I loved having deer run alongside us between the trail and the river. I was blessed to see a peacock near the road. And I caught my breath as two beavers in my path darted into a hole underneath the road just as I was about to hit them. That time I thought I was going to lose control of the bike and end up on the road myself, but I didn't.

As I was encountering these amazing animals and conversing with God, I would ask Him why He seemed to be increasing the number and kinds of animals I saw. Over time I learned several things:

- the more we find pleasure in Him, the more it pleases Him to bless us;
- when He made the earth and its inhabitants, He could have made just enough to make it functional; but God made it beautiful and adventurous for our pleasure; and
- the earth is His footstool,[32] so when I love, appreciate and am thankful for nature (God's creation), I am worshipping at His feet.

Because I sought to know more about my heavenly Father, God showed me more about Him. When I lacked wisdom about His creation, about Him and about how He wishes to relate to us, all I had to do was ask. He freely and beautifully taught me, and by teaching me, He helped me become more like Him, drawing me closer to Him as I began to see and appreciate the beauty of His creation.

In addition to teaching by His Word, and giving us wisdom when we ask for it, God also teaches us through our experiences. The above story about what I learned while training for a two-hundred-mile bike ride is not only an example of God's teaching me because I asked for wisdom but also an example of His teaching me by experience.

The process of training and becoming a long-distance rider was a wonderful experience. God also teaches us to be more like Him in our trials. The apostle Paul taught the church in Rome to glory in tribulations.[33] Doing so develops patience, hope and God's love in our hearts.[34] These are all Christ-like characteristics. In fact, the apostle James encouraged the church to be joyful when encountering the trials and temptations of life because they work patience in us, making us complete, needing nothing.[35]

As I write this, my husband and I are working on the mission field in Costa Rica. In 2019 when we were preparing to move here, after a wonderful time of being confident in God's calling and receiving multiple confirmations, we hit a time of trials. These trials ranged from concerns about our family, to attacks on our health, to financial matters. The trials made us wonder if we had misunderstood. *Had God called us at all?* The longer the trials lasted, the more God's hand became obvious. He was teaching us to be flexible and to trust Him. Things on the mission field would not be as we expected them to be, but we needed to be flexible enough to roll with whatever came our way, and we needed to trust Him through every experience. I can't say we counted it all joy when we were going through the trials, yet we are now very happy God taught us these lessons. We would not have been prepared for this experience had we not been conformed into His likeness through those trials.

Like a good Father, God provides all we need to be like Him. He provides Christ as an example, teaches us through His Word and answers our requests for wisdom. Through His Holy Spirit, God develops in us the fruit of the Spirit.[36]

It is no coincidence that love is listed first in the fruit of the Spirit. It is common knowledge that nutrition labels on food packages list the ingredients in order from most to least. Although every part of the fruit of the Spirit is equally important, I believe love is listed first because without it, the remaining content of the fruit of the Spirit is not possible. We must love before we can have joy and peace, or be patient, gentle, meek, and self-controlled. To be like Christ, we must love. But God does not leave us alone to strive to be like Christ on our own. Instead, just like we inherit both physical and nonphysical characteristics of our parents, we also acquire from God the fruit of the Spirit as we grow in our walk with God and live according to His Spirit.

There are also other characteristics of Christ that we inherit, and we can find them if we read God's Word with an eye open to seeing characteristics of Christ that are evident in our lives. As an example, one morning not long ago I was doing my daily prayer and Bible reading when Mark 10:1 caught my attention. It reads, "And He arose from thence, and cometh into the coasts of Judaea by the farther side of Jordan: and the people resort unto him again; and as He was wont, He taught them again." Jesus was wont to teach, meaning it was His habit, His customary behavior, it is what He did passionately. On that particular morning, I realized that I inherited a love and passion for teaching from my heavenly Father.

I, too, am very passionate about teaching. Many people have said I am a natural teacher. Not only do I love teaching God's Word, but I also just naturally teach when I communicate with people. It helped me in my career, first as an insurance underwriter and then as a corporate attorney. As I work on the mission field in Costa Rica, God has given me a passion to teach English to the Costa Rican people. Teaching is a huge part of my life, and just like Jesus was "wont to teach," I am wont to teach. I am confident you will also find characteristics of Christ that are in you if you read the Scriptures with an eye open for them.

As we acknowledge Christ's work in us, His characteristics grow in us. As we are adopted by God through Jesus Christ, He makes us acceptable to Him.[37] He transforms us to the image of Christ from glory to glory through His Spirit.[38] As we walk by the Spirit and the Spirit transforms us, we inherit through adoption the characteristics of Christ. We need not fear that we are just like our natural parents, who may not have been present or able to love us the way we needed. On the contrary, we can look at ourselves and see how God has fathered us. He provided an example for us and taught us through His Word, our experiences and our questions. We have grown in the fruit of the Spirit and inherited His characteristics of love, joy, peace, longsuffering, gentleness, goodness, faith, meekness, temperance. And, yes, people will be able to see that we have our Father's eyes!

Contemplate How God Helped You Become Christ-Like

- Can you see incidents in your own life in which God fathered you by helping you become Christ-like and grow into a responsible, loving, mature person?

_____

_____

_____

_____

_____

- What are some difficult, if not downright terrible events in your life that God worked together for your good as you loved Him and sought His purpose in your life? How did these result in your becoming more Christ-like?

Hey Dad, It's Me!

_____
_____
_____
_____
_____

- Is there one characteristic of Jesus you love and find easy to incorporate into your own life? What is it?

_____
_____
_____
_____
_____

- What is the toughest characteristic of Jesus to emulate? Make that a matter of prayer and ask God to help you improve in that area. If you can't think of something, ask God to search your heart and reveal to you where you need to improve and to help you do so.

_____
_____
_____
_____
_____

Write these things down for further prayerful contemplation. Let God show you how He has fathered you as you read the next chapter about His unconditional love.

3

Unconditional Love:

He Loves You with an Everlasting Love

Hey Dad, it's me!

I have been thinking about you a lot lately and considering what I want to say to you next. Please remember my purpose for reaching out to you is to assure you that you do not need to feel guilty about me and the fact that you were not present in my life. Although you may not be able to understand, anything you could have done in my life God far exceeded, so the topic today is love.

Many years ago, I sent you an email that contained what may have been the first time I expressed my feelings about our relationship. Here's what I said:

Dad, you have been on my mind a lot lately. And I guess I'll take this opportunity to tell you that I love you! We have both tried to make a father/daughter relationship over the years, but it has been difficult for a variety of reasons; mostly because we live so far apart and because we don't have the memories of a lifetime together to draw upon. As we both grow older, it becomes more and more difficult to build that relationship.

I ended the email with, "From me, the one who always wanted to be 'your little girl!'" Even as I write this now, Dad, that desire to be your little girl overwhelms me.

Do you remember how you responded? Here's what you said:

> *Thanks, Julie. I think under the circumstances we have done pretty well in our relationship. I agree with all you say. We haven't burdened each other and we always have known when it comes down to the nitty gritty, we will be there for each other.*

I have kept this email exchange all of these years.

Somehow, I think you and I have differing definitions of love. Apparently, you define it as not burdening each other but being there for each other in the nitty gritty. I define it as much more than that. I like what Oswald Chambers says about love.

> If human love does not carry a man beyond himself, it is not love. If love is always discreet, always wise, always sensible and calculating, never carried beyond itself, it is not love at all. It may be affection, it may be warmth of feeling, but it has not the true nature of love in it.[1]

Not burdening each other and being there for each other in the nitty gritty doesn't quite stand up to Oswald Chamber's definition. Some time ago I read *Bringing Up Girls: Shaping the Next Generation of Women* by James Dobson.[2] Dr. Dobson states, "Nearly all a woman does in her adult life is fueled by her longing to be delighted in, her longing to be beautiful, to be irreplaceable."[3] I think that is why I still cry when I think about being your little girl. In your absence I did not have the opportunity to be delighted in by you, at least not in the years I can remember. Even though you are not my legal father, my search for fatherly love, and being delighted in and thought to be beautiful and irreplaceable, leads me to you.

Why am I saying all of this? Because I want you to understand how God exceeded anything you could have been for me. Even if you were able to express a love that goes beyond yourself and delight in me as your daughter, the expression would have fallen short of the unconditional love my heavenly

Father has shown me. I know church, prayer and Bible reading have not been a regular part of your life, but it is important to me that you understand I believe the Bible is true and have strived to live my life according to it. I will go into that another time, but today I want you to realize how God has fathered me.

King David proclaimed in one of his psalms that God is a "father of the fatherless."[4] And God has certainly been that to me. The psalms also tell us that God delights in His children, of which I am one.[5] He satisfies my desire to be delighted in!

The Bible also contains a very interesting book which has been interpreted in a number of different ways. Scholars view the Song of Solomon as either a collection of love poems or a drama expressing love between two people. But some people interpret it as an allegory describing the love of Christ for His church. His church is not a building or a particular religious organization. Instead, each of His children make up His church. I am a part of His church. Therefore, I can accept the expressions of love in the Song of Solomon as applicable to me. As such, I learn that God finds me beautiful.[6] He satisfies my desire to be found beautiful, no matter how I look at any particular time!

The bottom line is that God loves me with an everlasting, unconditional love![7] I think the apostle John said it best: "See what great love the Father has lavished on us, that we should be called children of God! And that is what we are!"[8]

Do you remember when I called you and told you I was pregnant? This was after you co-signed the loan for a car for me because I was getting a divorce. And then I became pregnant from another relationship. You were kind and tried to conceal your disappointment. I certainly appreciated that. I was pretty disappointed in myself. I feared your love for me had reached its limits.

But do you know what my heavenly Father did? First, He patiently waited until I turned my eyes to Him. He did not want me to be lost but wanted me to return to Him in repentance.[9] Then He assured me I need not fear because I would not be put to shame, and I would forget the shame of my youth.[10] I can remember the day I was lying on my bed and reached for my Bible, which I had not done for some time. And there He was, assuring me with His Word again, drawing me back into His unconditional love, and I knew this baby and I were going to be fine.

Dad, you have no reason to feel guilty. I am loved with a greater love than you or anyone else ever could have shown me. God fathered me. Thus, I have been fathered by the greatest Father alive!

From me, the one who always wanted to be "your little girl!"

Julie McGhghy

The Love of Our Heavenly Father

Well, that was a difficult letter to write to my dad! Did I long for the love of a father for many years of my life? Definitely! Did I make mistakes that are statistically common among young women who grow up without the love of a father? Absolutely! I looked for love from all the wrong people. I made mistakes. As a result, I became pregnant with a little girl who longed to meet her biological father. The circumstances of her birth were unspeakable, yet God is faithful to work all things together for good when we love Him and are called according to His purpose.[11] What a blessing my beautiful daughter is in my life. I am grateful God lovingly turned unspeakable circumstances into one of my life's greatest treasures.

Was my dad, who was absent for the majority of my life, able to love me the way Oswald Chambers described love? No. Unfortunately, there are many fathers who are physically present in their children's lives who are unable to extend love to anyone beyond themselves. But God is able to extend love to His children . . . and He did!

Jesus suffered and died for us on the cross so that we may have eternal life.[12] What a demonstration of a love that reaches beyond Himself! That love exceeds what any earthly father could offer his children! And that love extends to you and me.

Although nothing can exceed the sacrifice made by Jesus on our behalf, God continues showing His love to us by calling us His children.[13] How amazing is that? He is not just talking to the church corporately. He is talking to you and me individually. You and I are God's children if we have received Him and believed in His name.[14] The mere act of calling us children demonstrates God's love, a love that goes beyond Himself.

And it keeps getting better! We aren't just children, but we are heirs with Jesus Christ.[15] What does that mean? It means that everything Christ has a right to, we also have a right to because we are joint heirs with Him. He gives us His glory,[16] His riches[17] and all things.[18] That inheritance is everlasting because it is incorruptible, undefiled, and it does not fade away.[19]

We Don't Disappoint God by Making Mistakes

Did God ever turn His back on me when I made mistakes? Absolutely not! One thing I have learned over the years is that God is never disappointed in us. My mistakes may have disappointed my dad, but they didn't disappoint God, and He didn't withhold His love from me because of them. His love is unconditional.

To disappoint is to fail to satisfy the hope, desire or expectation of someone. We learn from the apostle Paul that disappointment contains an element of surprise. Paul explained in his letter to the church in Galatia that he marveled they were so soon removed from him.[20] "Marvel" means to be surprised and astonished. Paul is expressing to the Galatians his surprise and disappointment that they were deserting their faith in the gospel of Christ and moving toward other teachings.

Surprise is part of disappointment. When we don't expect people to perform a certain way, we aren't surprised when they don't. Therefore, we aren't disappointed because we weren't expecting anything from them. As an example, consider asking your husband to pick up a jacket from the cleaners because you would like to wear it to church. Your husband explains that he cannot do so. When he doesn't pick it up, you are not disappointed because you are not surprised; but if he told you he would pick it up and fails to do so, then you are disappointed because you are surprised that he didn't do what you asked and what he said he would do.

So, when we make bad decisions in our lives, do we disappoint God? No. What does God expect of us? He expects us to believe on the name of Jesus and to love one another.[21] He expects no more of us but to believe and love because He knows we are human.[22]

In order for God to be disappointed, He must also be surprised. Can we surprise God? He is omniscient, all-knowing.[23] Since He knows us so intimately, He certainly is not surprised by anything we think, say or do, or fail to do. We do not disappoint God when we make mistakes. He does not withhold His love from us. His love is unconditional.

Just as I had disappointed my dad by becoming pregnant after my divorce, we all disappoint our parents and ourselves on occasion. We may feel like our parents don't love us because of their disappointment in us. But no matter what we do, God loves each of us. Even when I made some pretty bad decisions, living in a way that is inconsistent with God's Word, He loved me and still does. He loves us all with an unconditional, everlasting love, and He exceeded the love my father could have had for me, even if he had been a regular part of my life.

Contemplate How God Has Loved You Unconditionally

I encourage you to look back over your life. Did you disappoint your parents? Yourself? Did you beat yourself up because you were certain you disappointed God? Well, you didn't. God was there loving you, caring for you and fathering you all along. He sent His Son as a sacrifice for your sins. He calls you His child, and He made you a joint heir with Christ. He is not disappointed in you. God loves you with an everlasting, unconditional love.

- Reflect on some things you have done that caused you to feel disapproval from your parents and disappointment from God. Consider how God actually loved you through those situations.

- Identify some scriptures that speak God's unconditional love to you and commit one or two of them to memory. Pray them regularly, thanking God for His unconditional love.

Write these things down for further prayerful contemplation. Let God show you how He has fathered you as you read the next chapter that distinguishes religion from Christianity.

4

Religion Versus Christianity:

How We Live the Difference

Hey Dad, it's me!

I miss you, Dad. I am thankful for this opportunity to share with you why you need not feel guilty about not being an active part of my life as I was growing up. What I really want you to understand is God fathered me in a way that was far greater than you or any other earthly father could have. And today I want to address something you said to me many years ago about going to church.

Several years ago, as you and I were talking on the phone, I shared that Mike and I had started going to a new church. I was pretty excited about the change because I felt I was learning more about God and how to have a close relationship with Him. Your response? "It's okay to go to church, as long as the church doesn't tell you how to live!" Oh, Dad. I felt like I had been punched in the stomach. I know you weren't meaning to hurt me. You were speaking out of love. It was one of the very few times in my life that you tried to give me advice. But it only illuminated how different we were and how little we knew each other.

As I mentioned in my last letter to you, I know church, prayer and Bible reading have not been a regular part of your life. Because I was not raised by parents who were committed to teaching me about God and regularly attending a church, Grandma did everything she could to ensure I was able to be in church when I wanted to be.

When I was in junior high school, Grandma began taking me to church on Wednesday evenings so I could be part of the youth group and the choir. I would walk to her house after school. We would eat dinner together and then go to church. The choir practiced on Wednesday nights, so I had an opportunity to develop friendships with Christian young people and to be with those friends. After church, Grandma would take me home.

From that time on church has almost always been part of my life. I learned about and experienced God's love. I learned how to love Him in return. Through church I learned how to live a Christian life.

Certainly, the churches I attended had certain doctrines and taught me to live according to those doctrines. But never did a church "tell me how to live." Religions tell you how to live, and I have never been part of a religion. Churches show you God's love and teach you how to walk with Him. Because I can see how God has loved me, and I can get to know Him and what pleases Him through reading the Bible, I voluntarily choose to live my life in a way that pleases Him. I choose to dress or not dress certain ways. I choose to go or not go to certain places. I choose to talk or not talk in certain ways. But the church never tells me how I must live. To do so would cross over to a religion, not a church, not Christianity.

Consider the "Ten Commandments" in the Old Testament as a simple example. Through these commandments God taught His people how He wanted them to live because He loved them and wanted to protect them. When we read the New Testament, we learn that God wants to give us abundant life. Living according to the Ten Commandments helps us live that abundant life because it helps us develop deep, healthy relationships with God, our parents and other people. It also protects us from the emotional and mental burdens of living deceitfully and striving to "keep up with the Joneses." This is how God loves and protects us and how we learn to live when we regularly attend church.

Now consider religions. Religions look at adherence to the Ten Commandments or another book of rules as necessary to go to heaven. By obeying them and complying with many other requirements, people practicing religion think they earn eternal life or some other reward. Religions tell their people how to live.

Dad, I have never been part of a religion. But I do strive to live a Christian life according to the teachings of the Bible, and my church helps me do that. I am thankful for the teachings and guidance I receive from my church. And I strive to teach others about God's love and what pleases Him in order for them to enter into a relationship with God and live an abundant life. So, Dad, in response to your concern voiced so many years ago, I don't go to a church that tells me how to live. I go to a church that loves me enough to teach me how to develop a close, intimate relationship with God in order to have abundant life.

From me, the one who always wanted to be "your little girl!"

The Difference Between Religion and Christianity

I remember so clearly the day Dad and I had the discussion I described in my letter to him. I knew Dad well enough at the time to know he didn't go to church. Yet, I had never heard him talk about church. And when he made that statement, "It's okay to go to church, as long as the church doesn't tell you how to live," I heard resentment in his voice. I was so shocked by the statement that I couldn't ask him to explain what he meant or why he felt that way. Honestly, I didn't even know what to say. So, I changed the subject to something less emotional. After all, I wasn't accustomed to hearing such emotion in Dad's voice.

Even though in the above letter I gave Dad a simple explanation and an example between religion and Christianity, I recognize the difference isn't that black and white. Even when striving to live a Christian life, it is easy to fall into an erroneous, legalistic view. But before going into that, let's first revisit what a religion is.

I particularly like the following definition: "Religion is humanity's attempt to reach out to God or the sacred or divine. It involves human effort to become acceptable to God or to give meaning to one's life."[1]

Mike Mazzalongo explains the basic tenets of a number of religions in *What Other Religions Teach About Salvation*."[2] He distinguishes them from Christianity by who carries the responsibility for obtaining salvation, however salvation is expressed by the particular religion. Recognizing there are many different beliefs and traditions of each religion, he boils down the primary requirements of each religion to a simple description. Consider Islam and Hinduism as examples.

Under Islam, Mr. Mazzalongo explains, a person accesses salvation by practicing and repeating the five pillars of Islam: 1) Confessing that Muhammad is the Prophet; 2) Fasting; 3) Pilgrimage; 4) Giving alms; and 5) Praying five times a day. It is the responsibility of the person to obtain salvation through these actions. Interestingly, Mr. Mazzalongo notes that faithfully practicing the pillars is not sufficient to ensure salvation. Allah may still find the person deficient. The only way to obtain salvation with certainty under Islam is to die through jihad. Again, salvation is obtained through the actions of the person.

Hinduism is another example of a religion. Under Hinduism, Mr. Mazzalongo explains, the goal is to "merge with Brama" (or Brahman as discussed in other writings about Hinduism) as opposed to spending an eternity in a place called heaven. A person does this by eliminating evil in his or her life until he or she is pure enough to merge with Brama. This is not generally accomplished in a single lifetime. Therefore, each person seeks purity while living a succession of lives through reincarnation. The merger with Brahman ends the cycle of reincarnation.[3]

A more thorough writing about Hinduism explains the eternal duties of "honesty, refraining from injuring living beings, patience, forbearance, self-restraint, virtue, and compassion, among others."[4] However, it is impossible to boil the beliefs of Hinduism down to a simple statement because, as the writer explains, Hinduism "has no ecclesiastical order, no unquestionable religious authorities, no governing body, no prophet(s) nor any binding holy book."[5] The list of these duties remains consistent with Mr. Mazzalongo's assertion that the burden of achieving the final goal under the religion lies with the person seeking that goal.

So, how do these religions differ from Christianity? According to Mr. Mazzalongo, "Christianity is the only religion where the offer and burden for accomplishing salvation rests solely with God, and man can do nothing on his own to deserve or to accomplish his salvation. Salvation from a Christian perspective is possible and available to all."[6]

The apostle Paul makes it clear to the church in Ephesus that we are saved by grace through faith, and not by our own efforts.[7] Generally, Christians do not live according to the Bible because they are trying to earn salvation. Instead, we live according to biblical teachings because we love God and want to please Him. However, because we are human, in our own minds we sometimes blur the line between adopting Jesus's teachings out of love and out of obligation to earn salvation. That is when it becomes difficult to recognize the difference between a religion and going to a church that "tells you how to live" as Dad apparently experienced.

Living the Difference

If I am living consistently with the teachings of the Bible, what difference does it make whether I do so as an obligation to obtain salvation (religion) or out of love and deep relationship with Jesus? Isn't the end result the same--spending eternity in heaven? Maybe, but likely not. Let me explain.

First, consider why Jesus died for you. "For God so loved the world, that he gave his only begotten Son, that whosoever believeth in him should not perish, but have everlasting life."[8] Jesus died for you and me because He loves us. And He suffered the anguish and atrocities of a Roman crucifixion in order to reconcile us, bringing us back into relationship with God.[9] He didn't do this just so He could love us. No, he wanted a relationship with us, a two-way relationship built on love.

Being in a two-way relationship with us was so important to God that three of the four Gospel writers recorded Jesus's words explaining the greatest commandment, "Thou shalt love the Lord thy God with all thy heart, and with all thy soul, and with all thy mind."[10] This commandment did not originate in the New Testament with Jesus. He was quoting the greatest commandment given directly from God to Moses in the Old Testament.[11] Even in the Old Testament, God was teaching His people how to live an abundant life, observing these practices "that it may be well with thee, and that ye may increase mightily."[12]

What does this look like? It goes beyond just adhering to the Ten Commandments, the letter of the law as opposed to its intent. As an example, the Ten Commandments do not address fasting. The Day of Atonement was "the single prescribed occasion for fasting," but the validity of it "ceased when Jesus made the once-for-all sacrifice on the cross."[13] Yet, many people today continue fasting. Why? Because they love the Lord and want to serve Him completely.

In Scripture, there are many reasons to fast, including mourning,[14] seeking God's will when making decisions and appointing leaders,[15] facing challenging or dangerous situations,[16] receiving clear instruction from God,[17] humbling oneself and asking for God's mercy[18] and before beginning a ministry.[19] Although fasting goes beyond the requirements in Scripture, people who fast out of their love for God do so to draw closer to Him, know His will in their lives and seek His protection and mercy. This is part of the relationship God is seeking when He asks us to love Him with all our hearts, with all our souls and with all our minds.

But there is another way to apply biblical teachings to our lives. Some people strive to do all the Bible teaches, but they do so in order to obtain salvation. This is called "legalism" and gives Christianity the appearance of a religion. It connects a person's actions with achieving salvation or righteousness. When living legalistically, the person fears violating any of the commands and teachings of the Bible because doing so would lead to losing his or her salvation. And they don't apply this view only to their own salvation. In the book *Words of Endearment: The Ten Commandments as a Revelation of God's Love*, Dr. William Coker, Sr. explains the legalists of today are like the Pharisees in the New Testament, waiting around "ready to blast anyone who broke the Law."[20] He further explains legalists "make life miserable for themselves and everybody else."[21] This is what Dad likely experienced that caused him to warn me against going to a church that tells me how to live.

Let's return to our example of fasting. Both in the Old Testament and the New Testament God confronted people for fasting for the wrong reasons.

In Isaiah 58, God corrected the people who were fasting in order to make their voices heard, taking delight in approaching God for the appearance of doing so.[22] He described the incorrect purposes for their fasting, "for strife and debate, and to smite with the fist of wickedness."[23] This was not a fast that was pleasing to the Lord but rather was one the people performed in order to appear righteous.

In the parable of the Pharisee and the publican, Jesus provoked the Pharisees, the religious leaders of His day, to distinguish the difference between relying upon their own actions to obtain righteousness and humbly approaching God.[24] He told a story about two men who went into the temple to pray: one was a Pharisee and the other a tax collector. Tax collectors were viewed by the Jews as the vilest of sinners because they worked for Rome, and out of their own greed and desire for material comfort, they collected more money from the Jews than was owed to Rome.

In this parable the Pharisee compared himself to other men, including the tax collector.[25] While praying he proclaimed his own righteousness. Further, he recited his own routines of fasting twice a week and tithing on everything he owned as proof of his own righteousness.[26]

In contrast, the tax collector humbly approached God, not even lifting his eyes to heaven, and asked God for mercy as he acknowledged his sin.[27] Jesus concluded that it was the tax collector, not the Pharisee, that was justified, meaning he was forgiven and righteous.[28]

The religious people in the Old Testament and the Pharisees in the New Testament both fasted to attain their own righteousness. They did not do it out of love for God. They were not able to achieve righteousness through their own legalistic approach to God. On the other hand, the tax collector loved God and humbly approached Him, asking for mercy and forgiveness, recognizing God is the source of salvation, not himself. He received, as a free gift of grace, the salvation of the Lord.

Even today some Christians fear losing their salvation if they violate any of the Ten Commandments, other biblical teachings or rituals established by their churches. I was married to my husband for many years before I realized that he approached his relationship with God legalistically, following a list of dos and don'ts. Notwithstanding, at the time he would not have recognized it as such or called it that; he would acknowledge his relationship with God was one of obedience . . . only. He did not feel the love of God. He certainly didn't feel the joy of the Lord. But he did what he was taught to do growing up in order to have salvation, which included regular church attendance,[29] tithing,[30] loving one another[31] and a myriad of other dos and don'ts. He couldn't feel the joy of the Lord because He was so concerned about violating any of the rules he had been taught to obey. To him, at the time, serving the Lord was a duty, an obligation and to do otherwise would mean spending eternity in hell. Obviously, he did not want to do that.

Thankfully, for both my husband and me, he came to understand the love God has for him. He began to realize there is joy in serving the Lord, and unintentional missteps, those that would technically be considered sin, do not and will not sever his relationship with God.[32] He even began understanding that he gained strength through the joy of the Lord.[33] It was only after this realization that he was able to love the Lord and see Him in every area of our lives, the good and the bad, and be thankful.

How we approach God and seek our salvation does make a difference. We can never do anything to deserve God's grace, mercy and salvation. Approaching God legalistically hinders our goal of spending eternity with God because it focuses on our own ability to achieve salvation; and as human beings, we do not have the strength to obey every biblical teaching without the help of the Holy Spirit and the joy of the Lord. And legalism will not grow our love for Him. On the other hand, out of God's great mercy He will grant us salvation when we come to Him humbly, confessing our sins and adhering to the plan of salvation established in His Word. Doing so results in our learning how to love the Lord with all our hearts, minds and souls and choosing our actions accordingly. Are there dos and don'ts in the Bible? Of course there are, but they are given to us by a loving Father who knows what we need in order to live an abundant life. Adopting and adhering to those dos and don'ts in our own lives because we love the Lord is the proper approach to our relationship with God and will lead to an abundant life, a deeper love for God and an eternity with Him.

What's a Father to Do?

It may seem odd that I include this discussion in a book about seeing how God fathers us. But our fathers have a great deal to do with how we view God. According to Jay Payleitner in his book *52 Things Daughters Need From Their Dads*, fathers have "been given the responsibility to protect our families and provide them with opportunities to fulfill God's call on their lives here on earth."[34] Dr. Meg Meeker in her book *Strong Fathers, Strong Daughters: 10 Secrets Every Father Should Know* explains that children turn to their fathers for answers about God whether the father believes or disbelieves in God.[35] And if he believes, the child will want to know what God is like.[36]

For me, even had Dad been active in my life as I grew up, he would not have been able to point me to God. His resentment of the church would certainly have been passed on to me. But God had a different plan for my life. God used my grandmother to introduce me to church and to connect me to the body of Christ in the church. Through those connections, both with young people my own age and adults, I developed a relationship with God.

God draws us to him. Jesus taught the crowds that sought Him that no one can come to Him unless God draws him.[37] Dr. Curt Dodd explains that God draws us through His Word, His people, His Spirit and our circumstances.[38] God fathered me by drawing me to Him. He first drew me through my grandmother. She would speak to me about God's love and make sure I could be active in church on Sundays and Wednesdays. Then He drew me through the people in the church who also showed me God's love and instilled in me a love for His Word. As I heard and read God's Word, I discovered more about God's character and how to draw close to Him. And His Word equipped me to do His will.[39] Without God's Word, I would never have been equipped to do His work in Costa Rica.

God also draws us through the Holy Spirit by convicting us of our sin. Jesus explained to His apostles that once He had departed from the earth, the Holy Spirit would come and convict us of our sin and demonstrate God's judgment of sin and righteousness.[40] It is through the Holy Spirit, not Dad's teaching, that I learned about my sin and need for God.

Dr. Meeker explains the media often treats belief in God and active participation in worshipping at church or temple as being "repressive, antiquated, unrealistic, unintelligent, and maybe even psychologically harmful to kids."[41] Dad probably would have agreed with this view since he felt churches tell you how to live. But "the statistical evidence says something very different."[42]

Studies on adolescents indicate that "a belief in God and an active participation in worshipping at church or temple, going to youth groups," and being involved in Christian (termed "religious" by the studies) activities is protective of kids.[43] Dr. Meeker presents a long list of the positive impact active participation in church activities has on young people as shown in a number of those studies. Consider these few examples:

- Helps kids stay away from drugs, sexual activity and smoking;[44]
- Gives kids moral guidance and feelings of mental and psychological security;[45] and
- Furthers their maturity as they transition from childhood through adolescence.[46]

Dad was not equipped to protect me and provide me with opportunities to fulfill God's call on my life despite having the responsibility to do so. He could not have done it even if he had been an active part of my life as I grew up. But God was there to father me and provided all the guidance I needed to find Him. Don't get me wrong, church did not keep me from all of the usual struggles of youth. Yet, God was always there as a good Father guiding me down the right path. And when I took another path, I always knew God would be there when I returned. And I did return.

Contemplate How God Has Drawn You to Him

I encourage you to prayerfully consider your relationship with God and the church.

- Are you striving to live according to biblical teaching out of a fear of losing your salvation if you don't? If so, search out scriptures about God's grace and include them in your prayers, thanking God for His grace. Some good scriptures about grace include the ones mentioned in this chapter: Ephesians 1:3-6, Ephesians 2:8-9, and 2 Corinthians 8:9.

- Are you striving to live according to God's Word out of a deep love for your Savior who paid such a great price for your soul? Look back on your life and see how God has fathered you by drawing you to Him and His truth.

_____

_____

_____

_____

_____

_____

Write these things down for further prayerful contemplation. Let God show you how He has fathered you as you read the next chapter about God being our authority figure.

5

Authority Figure:

He Is the Source of Our Support and Guidance

Hey Dad, it's me!

Today I am thinking about authority. I am sure that sounds odd. Don't most kids buck against authority? I suppose that is true, but there were times in my life when I needed an authority figure. I needed someone I could run to.

Certainly, you were there when I was going through the divorce as I mentioned in a previous letter. I called you for help because I was in California, alone, with no transportation. You helped me by co-signing a loan for a car. I was so thankful for that financial help. Yet there were other times in my life when I needed guidance, support and a helping hand.

As I think about it today, one such situation was when I was in high school and contemplating going to college. Oh, I wanted to go to college so badly. Yet no one in my family had been to college or had any idea how to direct me to pursue a college education. I wasn't a student that caught the guidance counselors' attention at school. No one sought me out to encourage me and help me understand what I needed to do as a student to prepare for the college application process. I clearly did not build a high school transcript or participate in extra-curricular activities that would have positioned me to complete an application that was attractive to college recruiters.

I remember one of the few times in my life that I sat around your table with your second family. Your son told a story about how you had helped him make a last-minute decision about what college to attend. I assume you had encouraged him to be a good student while he was in high school and helped him prepare for the whole college application process. He was probably involved in extra-curricular activities. And he had an attractive college application.

As I recall the story, multiple colleges accepted his application and offered scholarships. He had accepted the invitation of one school, yet as he prepared to leave for college, he had a gnawing feeling that he should go to another one. One week prior to the start of the semester he shared his concerns with you. You gave him the courage to be guided by his instincts and to contact that second college. At the last minute, he was able to switch colleges and go to the one his instincts lead him to. As he recounted that story at your dining room table, he expressed how thankful he was for your guidance and how you empowered him to make a good decision, even if it was a bit late in the process. On that day, at your table I thought, "What a beautiful story. Would my life be different if I had had that kind of love and guidance?"

Although I wish I had experienced that type of guidance from you as my authority figure, you do not have to feel guilty about not being there guiding me through such times in my life. God filled that role. I won't act like I opened the Bible and it said, "Go to this college." Nor did anyone come to me and tell me, "Thus saith the Lord ...." But God guided me using friends who had parents guiding them.

One day at the lunch table at school a friend began talking about all of the college brochures she was getting. These were all from Christian colleges. I asked why she was getting them, and she explained how she signed up for information and Christian colleges started recruiting her. That was something I had never heard about. I went home that evening and filled out a sign-up card she had shared with me from a Christian magazine and mailed it. Soon I was receiving college brochures also.

I still didn't know how to proceed, but I began seriously contemplating a college education. Due to some changes in my home life, I was not able to pursue college at that time. But the dream was percolating in my head. While completing my last year of high school, God gave me direction that I would use later in my life. Ultimately, I completed a bachelor's degree with Magna Cum Laude honors and, much later in life, completed a Juris Doctorate with

Cum Laude honors. God transformed this C-average high school student into a serious college and graduate student capable of graduating with honors.

Dad, I am not saying your guidance wouldn't have helped me develop into a good student. But I am saying there is no reason to feel guilty that you weren't there, because God filled in the gaps. Between high school and college, I learned more about God and began striving to live according to His Word. The first scripture I chose to help guide me was 1 Corinthians 10:31, which states, "whatsoever ye do, do all to the glory of God."[1] By striving to glorify Him in all things, I learned to study and apply myself to my studies in order to earn good grades. That was the guidance I needed to achieve the honors I received.

From me, the one who always wanted to be "your little girl!"

Parental Authority

I know a dear, sweet young woman whom I have watched grow up since infancy. Like all teenagers, she was very attached to her cell phone and the Internet. Unfortunately, there are many predators on the Internet, and she fell prey to a few. But what really amazed me as I watched her grow was how she responded to her parents' efforts to protect her.

This young woman frequently expressed strong displeasure about how her parents were over-protective and monitored her cell phone and Internet use. Even in her late teens, she had a curfew for turning off the phone. Her parents monitored her whereabouts through her phone whenever she left the house. This didn't set well with this young woman.

On the other hand, whenever the young woman got into difficult situations she didn't know how to handle, she would begin acting out or being careless with her phone so her parents would discover what was going on and intervene to help her. This is a good example of the love/hate relationship we as human beings have with authority.

Dr. Meeker explains, "It is a fundamental principle of human behavior that having an authority makes us feel good."[2] That sounds odd when you consider how many of us have grown up resisting authority, not only during our high school years but, for some of us, all of our lives. By the time my own three children made it through adolescence, I had come to the conclusion that God gave us the adolescent years so that at the end of them the children would be ready to leave the nest and the parents would be ready to let them fly! And some thirty years later, I still believe that as I watch my grandchildren go through adolescence.

Dr. Meeker further explains what she means by feeling good about having an authority figure.

While instinctively we want to buck it [authority], when the sky falls in, we run to it. When confronted by any problem, any challenge, any mess that we can't get ourselves out of, we want someone who has answers, someone who can offer support, someone who can offer a helping hand and who knows what to do.[3]

This is exactly what the dear, sweet young woman was doing when she found herself in situations she could not handle. She didn't directly run to her parents for help; instead, she acted out in ways that caught their attention, or she would do something that would cause them to demand that she hand over her phone so they could look through it and determine what was going on. This young lady, while almost constantly bucking her parents' authority, treasured the safety of it when she needed it. When she got in a mess she couldn't handle, she went to her parents. And her parents always helped her work through the messes.

God's Authority

When we consider God's authority, we often consider His sovereignty. God declared to Jeremiah, "Behold, I *am* the Lord, the God of all flesh: is there any thing too hard for me?"[4] And Israel's King David proclaimed God's power in prayer when he prayed, "Thine, O Lord, *is* the greatness, and the power, and the glory, and the victory, and the majesty: for all *that is* in the heaven and in the earth *is thine*: thine *is* the kingdom, O Lord, and thou are exalted as head above all."[5] Even Job, after he had been corrected by the Lord, repented and proclaimed, "I know that thou canst do every *thing*, and *that* no thought can be withholden from thee."[6] Recognizing this great power of the Lord in both heaven and earth, we can be hindered from considering Him as an active Father in our lives. We know the power and authority He has. Regardless, when we need help, guidance and support, we often neglect to think of Him as the Father we can run to.

God is more than our Father by title. He actively fathers us. He is more than a ruler with an iron fist. He has power and authority to do all things. But what does He want to do? He wants to father us.

Jesus beckons us to come to Him when we are exhausted from our labors, and I dare say from our striving to keep everything in our lives together![7] Like a good father, He wants to help us find rest from our burdens. How often do we run hither and yon seeking other people's guidance, support and help when we encounter something we don't know how to handle?

It wasn't long after Trisha was born that she became very sick. She struggled with respiratory issues. When she was an infant, she slept in a crib next to my bed. When she slept, she often couldn't breathe. I would wake up because of her horrible gasping and coughing. I would have to hold her upright so she could breathe. This happened every time I laid her down, even if just for naps. She could not breathe when lying horizontally.

As an inexperienced mom, I sought advice and help from anyone who would listen to my questions. Doctors weren't much help. Eventually she fell into a routine of being in the hospital for two weeks in an oxygen tent to clear up her lungs, then be at home and in childcare for two weeks until the problem became so severe that she was put back in the hospital. This two weeks in and two weeks out of the hospital cycle continued for months. To take her to childcare, which I had to do because I was a single mom and had to work two jobs to pay the medical bills, I had to carry two diaper bags. One was full of the medicines she had to take while the other had her normal formula, diapers and extra clothing.

During this time, did I take my problems to my heavenly Father? No. Like many people, I ran from person to person seeking advice; I took her from doctor to doctor trying to find an answer. I did all of this while I worked two jobs. I was exhausted. But at the time, like so many of us, I did not think to go to my heavenly Father for guidance, support and a helping hand. I did not seek the rest that He promised in His Word. Yet, He was there beckoning me all along.

God wants us to come to Him with our needs. He wants us to cast all of our cares on Him.[8] It is by placing our cares on His shoulders that we experience the peace that passes all human understanding.[9] This is the rest He longs to give us.

It wasn't until many years later that I learned how much I can trust the Lord, and how by doing so, He would direct me to the help and rest I needed. Again, it was by caring for my own children that I learned to trust Jesus.

What I am going to share now is very sensitive and will be hard for many to understand. I wouldn't have understood someone else's similar story if I had not experienced this myself with my own child. And please know that I have my now-adult child's permission to tell this story.

My son, Jason, was a very intelligent child. In the second grade he was reading at the fifth-grade level. In elementary school when he took standardized tests, he scored at the ninety-ninth percentile rank. Of course, as parents, my husband and I were happy to see his hunger for learning. He often came home from school and went to our Encyclopedia Britannica to read more about a topic he had just learned about at school. But sometimes high intelligence is accompanied by social and emotional struggles. And that proved to be true for Jason.

One evening as I was cooking dinner, my ten-year-old daughter came to me and told me Jason was giving his things away because he planned to kill himself the next day. *What?* I remember being in utter disbelief, much like you probably are as you are reading this. How can a seven-year-old be hurting so badly that he wants to kill himself? And how does a seven-year-old plan such a thing. *This can't really be happening!*

I knew enough about the progress of depression and suicide through my college education to know that putting things in order, such as giving things away and making a plan were two of the last steps before attempting suicide. So, I took this very seriously.

After talking to Jason, consulting his school counselor and desperately crying out to God, my husband and I sought a child psychiatrist who confirmed Jason was struggling and was, in fact, having suicidal thoughts. We had to make the hardest decision of our lives at that time and since. We allowed the psychiatrist to admit Jason into an in-patient psychiatric hospital for thirty days. *Oh, God, how can this be happening? Lord, are we making the right decision? The risk of a wrong decision is too great, Lord. Oh, God, guide us!*

In the 1980s, even for adults, admitting you had an emotional problem was very controversial, especially in Christian circles. Well-meaning people would counsel you that you didn't need psychiatric help or medicine, you just needed more faith in God. With that kind of pressure, we didn't feel we could consult our pastor or church friends for support. Also, once the professionals determined Jason had a plan that certainly would have been successful, things moved so quickly that we didn't have time to contact anyone for spiritual counsel and support. If I remember correctly, Jason was admitted into the hospital the day after we learned about his plan.

I hope as you read this you are shocked and can't even imagine. A shocked reaction to this story would indicate you've never gone through something like this, which I pray is true. But we all have experiences in our lives that knock our feet right out from under us, and we don't know where to turn. That is what this experience was for us.

How did God father me through this time? He came to me through His Word. Shortly before all of this happened, our pastor had preached about the parable of the potter and the clay from Jeremiah 18. During the thirty days of hospitalization and three years of psychiatric care Jason needed, God kept bringing that parable back to me.

The word which came to Jeremiah from the Lord, saying, Arise, and go down to the potter's house, and there I will cause thee to hear my words. Then I went down to the potter's house, and, behold, he wrought a work on the wheels. And the vessel that he made of clay was marred in the hand of the potter: so he made it again another vessel, as seemed good to the potter to make *it*. Then the word of the Lord came to me, saying, O House of Israel, cannot I do with you as this potter? Saith the Lord. Behold, as the clay is in the potter's hand, so *are* ye in mine hand, O house of Israel.[10]

During that time, I had to let go and trust God. He was the potter. He was working in Jason, even at that young age, to make him the person He purposed him to be. He was working in me also. But in addition to being the potter, God was fathering both Jason and me, "But now, O Lord, thou *art* our father; we *are* the clay, and thou our potter; and we all *are* the work of thy hand."[11]

God guided us, helped us and supported us during this difficult time. He was the only One I could run to for help. Dad couldn't help me. Our pastor couldn't help me. My friends couldn't help me. Only God could provide the help, support and guidance I needed to get through that time. It was also during that period that I learned to trust that God would direct my paths as long as I acknowledged Him in all things.[12]

God was and is sovereign, but He is not unapproachable. He is our ultimate authority, and He loves us. He is there to help us and guide us through all life throws at us. Having His authority over us makes us feel good just as Dr. Meeker explained.

Contemplate How God Has Been Your Authority Figure

In this chapter I shared a couple of difficult situations I had to handle in my life. In one I ran to everyone but God for help even though He was there all along, wanting to father me as an authority figure, giving guidance, help and support.

In the second situation, I was so devastated I could turn to no one but God as my Father and authority figure. It was in the second situation that I grew in my relationship with God.

- Consider the very challenging times in your life. Was there a situation in which you ran hither and yon for help and never turned your eyes to God? Was there another one in which God was clearly there fathering you through it?

_____
_____
_____
_____
_____
_____

- How did you feel during each of these experiences?

_____
_____
_____
_____

- Which one resulted in more personal growth?

- Think of an example where God's authority in your life made you feel good as Dr. Meeker asserts.

Write these things down for further prayerful contemplation. Let God show you how He has fathered you as you read the next chapter about the boundaries God lovingly establishes.

6

Boundaries:

God's Loving Source of Security

Hey Dad, it's me!

I was driving down the road the other day and considered the lack of stripes on the road. Here in Costa Rica many of the roads are narrow, curvy and have no stripes delineating the lanes or edges of the roads. One might think this is most hazardous on narrow roads, especially at night or when it is raining, because it is difficult to see where to drive. But I have found it most hazardous on wider roads, generally those heavily traveled at higher speeds and wide enough for three or four lanes. A wide road with two-way traffic and no delineation of the lanes is quite hazardous. Why? Because drivers going both directions think they are in their own lanes, when they are actually taking a swath down the middle. Then other drivers squeeze to the side, making a road that was probably intended for two lanes into four lanes. When two vehicles going the opposite direction realize they are both in the same lane, there is no room to move over because there are cars in the "outside lanes." These roads without boundaries are often the making of a collision.

Why do I share this? Because it caused me to start thinking about parental boundaries. It's common knowledge that parents should set boundaries for their children. This is usually done easily enough when the children are young. Establishing routines of mealtime, bedtime and bath time is all pretty normal. These early boundaries give the child a sense of security by knowing what to expect and when to expect it.

As children grow, teaching them where they are allowed to play or to walk is all pretty normal. Parents teach them it is safe to play in the backyard or at a playground when within the sight of the supervising parent or grandparent. It's safe to walk on a sidewalk, but not on the street (or running through a parking lot!). These boundaries are all established because parents love their children and wish to protect them.

Boundaries are more difficult to set as children grow older. Parental boundaries are necessary to focus children on the things that help them mature into productive adults, such as applying themselves in school, possibly balancing school and a part-time job, budgeting and saving. Social boundaries are also important, teaching older children how to handle difficult situations--such as a trusted friend offering them drugs or inappropriate advances from someone of the opposite sex--and keeping all relationships respectful.

As I thought about parental boundaries, I realized you never had an opportunity to set boundaries for me. You couldn't set healthy curfews for me to keep me out of unseemly places and situations late at night. You couldn't show me that I was a young lady worthy of love and respect. You couldn't warn me about the difference between love and lust. But, Dad, you need not feel guilty about that.

God provided all the boundaries I needed in His Word. He fathered me by setting boundaries because He loves me and seeks to protect me.

Did I always comply with God's boundaries? No. Just like I wouldn't have always obeyed any boundaries you set for me. Like all children and teenagers, I pushed some of the boundaries. But I had a sense of the proper boundaries set forth in the Bible. When I got too far past them, I always knew where I could return for safety. God always extended His love and forgiveness to me and worked things out for my good when I messed things up.

When I was seventeen, disco was all the rage. There was a popular discotheque called Pogo's a few miles down the highway from where I lived. I was very active in a youth group and choir at a church that preached against dancing. In spite of that teaching, a number of the youth decided they wanted to go to Pogo's. They were going somewhat regularly with fake IDs. When they invited me to go along, I thought it sounded like fun. I found someone in our youth group who was old enough to get in but had no interest in going. I used her driver's license as ID. It worked. I got in. I spent the evening dancing with total strangers who had been drinking. I didn't drink and ordered only Coke. The line dances were innocent enough. But when a slow song was played, I suddenly found myself in the middle of the dance floor with a total stranger holding me way too tight and sweating all over me as we swayed to the music. Yuck! It was disgusting.

Fortunately, I realized I was not where I should have been. My friends and I left the place and I drove home. The next night, there was a fight at Pogo's that ended in a shooting in the parking lot.

God's Word set a boundary against lying ("Lie not one to another...," Colossians 3:9). He taught me to avoid the "fleshly lusts," which abounded with unrestraint in Pogo's ("Dearly beloved ... abstain from fleshly lusts...," 1 Peter 2:11). Complying with God's boundaries would have kept me out of Pogo's. But even though I challenged those boundaries, lying by using a fake ID and spending time in an establishment whose sole purpose was feeding the fleshly desires of young people, God protected me from the violence of the next evening. And He reinforced the boundaries against going to such places by ensuring I learned about that violence. I set my sights back on God and never returned to Pogo's or any place like it while I was underage.

God's boundaries are like the stripes in the road for me. As long as I followed them, I could safely travel through life. Without them I am confident I would have had many more collisions in my life.

From me, the one who always wanted to be "your little girl!"

The Purpose of Boundaries

Parents establish boundaries for their children because they love them and want them to be safe. And they want them to grow into respectable, productive adults.

Parents first focus on physical safety. When not at home, they prop pillows around flat, elevated surfaces they lay their baby on for a nap. They teach them not to play with electrical outlets or touch the hot stove. They put child locks on cabinets containing chemicals and other things that will harm their children.

As babies grow, parents set physical boundaries around their homes, putting up gates to keep them off the stairs or using a play pen to keep their babies in a safe location when the parents cannot keep their eyes on them, such as when cooking or tending to other children.

When children are walking well, physical boundaries are no longer effective. Parents must set boundaries by explaining what is safe and what is not. Don't cross the street without looking both ways first. Stay in the fenced backyard. Don't talk to strangers. If you get lost, go to a person in uniform for help.

Eventually, parents teach their children about respect, teaching them to respect their elders and speak respectfully. They guide them to stay away from cigarettes, drugs and sexual activity. And they teach them how to pursue a good future through education, working a part-time job and/or volunteering.

The purpose of all of these boundaries is to keep children safe and teach them how to interact in society. And parents set these boundaries because they love their children.

Dr. Meeker explains that children want to know the rules for living.[1] They don't just seek boundaries for their physical safety, but they also want to understand the moral rules to get along in society. Dr. Meeker encourages fathers to set clear moral guidelines.² It is not enough just to talk about the moral boundaries. The boundaries must be modeled. Fathers cannot effectively teach a child not to lie if they call into work sick the day after the Super Bowl game because the party got a little rowdy and continued late into the night. They can't teach the child to speak respectfully if they shout at the child and use curse words regularly. Children will learn more by the parents' actions than by their words.

The Source of Boundaries

If we grow up without a father to set boundaries or with one that fails to appropriately set and model the boundaries, we are not left to our own devices to figure it all out. Remember, God loves us even more than our own parents do. He wants us to grow into the person He has purposed us to be. He wants us safe from the physical and emotional harm caused by deceitful, greedy, promiscuous living. Therefore, He not only sets forth rules to live by in the Bible, but He also modeled them in the life of Jesus Christ. We have the example we need to know how to act according to the rules.

Just as teenagers often think their parents' rules are intended to keep them from having fun and living a full life, adults often think God's "commands" are intended for the same purpose. But God's intention is quite to the contrary. God wants us to have an abundant life free from guilt, shame, addictions and emotional scars that impair our efforts to attain all God has in store for us.

Dr. Coker explains that God's rules as articulated in the Ten Commandments "form the basis for a society that makes it possible to live together with respect."³ Dr. Coker affectionately calls the Ten Commandments "Words of Endearment" because they are an expression of God's love, not rules to adhere to in order to receive salvation.⁴

When people think of God's rules, they primarily think of the Ten Commandments set forth in Exodus 20:2-17 and Deuteronomy 5:6-21. They often refer to them as the "thou shalts" and "thou shalt nots" when discussing them a bit irreverently, pointing to them as chains on their freedom to live the lives they want to live. But as previously stated, God's reason for establishing them was quite to the contrary. Dr. Coker explains that God set a pattern of living to enable us to "live a full and abundant life," and adopting this pattern helps "maintain a whole and healthy society."[5]

Dr. Coker further explains God's boundaries don't affect only society as a whole but also individuals.[6] "When we live within His framework, life is pleasant. When we don't, there are consequences."[7]

I can remember the days of raising three teenagers. Each one challenged the boundaries we set in our home in different ways. One would never violate curfew but had a difficult time holding her tone at a respectful level. She knew the consequences for losing control of her tone when speaking with me. But there were times she deliberately just railed about whatever was on her mind. One time in the midst of such a railing, I asked her why she continued to do so when she knew the consequences would be sure and swift. She replied, "Because sometimes it feels so good to get it out that it's worth the consequences." Well, there you have it! At least she thought it out before violating the rules. But I dare say many people do not do the same.

Do Christians who enter into sexual relationships outside of marriage first consider the consequences of violating the sixth commandment, "Thou shalt not commit adultery"? So often we hear about a husband confessing his extra-marital sexual relationship to his wife only to state, "It wasn't planned. It just happened." If we accept that statement as true, then it clearly illustrates that there was no thought of the consequences before stepping into that relationship. And the consequences are extreme. Not only does the outside relationship destroy any trust that existed in the marriage, but it also frequently results in divorce, often in poverty, impacts the children's self-esteem and future, and it impacts both spouses' and the children's relationships with God. The husband often finds it difficult to return to God in repentance, thinking he has gone too far for God to forgive him. The wife and children find it difficult to trust God because He allowed this destruction of their family. These are the consequences God sought to protect us from when He established the boundary against adultery. This is just one example of a boundary God set for us out of His abundant love for us and desire to see us live a whole and healthy life.

Like a good father, God established healthy boundaries to protect us, His children. His love is shown in each and every one of the Ten Commandments. Yet, when asked by a lawyer which of these was the greatest commandment, Jesus boiled them down into two simple ones: 1) Love the Lord your God with all your heart, and with all your soul, and with all your mind; and 2) Love your neighbor as yourself.[8] God established the boundaries so we might live a life full of love in all of our relationships and in society as a whole. If we live inside His boundaries, we can discover all the good He has created for us, but if we go outside the boundaries, "we are going to introduce problems into society that destroy it, and it will destroy us in the process."[9]

Contemplate How God Fathered You by Establishing Boundaries

In this chapter I shared God's love in establishing boundaries for us to live by and His goal that we live a life full of love and the good things He created for us. The Ten Commandments are not the only boundaries God set for us. Jesus and His apostles established many guidelines in the New Testament that help us live the abundant life God planned for us. In what we call the Sermon on the Mount, Jesus so lovingly taught us there is more to living lovingly than merely adhering to the Ten Commandments.[10]

- Consider some of the boundaries your parents set for you. As you grew up, did you feel the love behind the boundary? If not, when did you discover the boundaries were established because your parents loved you and wanted to protect you?

___

- Consider how you viewed the Ten Commandments as you grew up. Did you view them as punitive in nature or as a loving boundary to ensure your safety and well-being?

___

- What are some instances when you pushed back against the boundaries set by your parents or set in the Bible? What were the consequences of breaking through those boundaries? Were the consequences merely administered as punishments or discipline by your parents, or can you see how the violation of the boundaries had more lasting impact on your life?

- Consider how God's boundaries helped you draw closer to Him and maintain loving relationships within your own family and friends.

Write these things down for further prayerful contemplation. Let God show you how He has fathered you as you read the next chapter about how God's protection goes beyond the boundaries.

7

Beyond the Boundaries:

God's Protection

Hey Dad, it's me!

After I wrote to you last about the boundaries God set for me, I began thinking about a father's protection. Boundaries proactively protect children from the routine dangers of life, such as drivers not being able to see children in parking lots or streets. But children also need protection from other dangers.

I am pretty confident most people consider it the father's role to protect his family, so I did a quick Internet search to confirm that thought. I was amazed at how many quotes I found about a father protecting his daughter. Here are a few of my favorites.

- "The most admirable thing ever has to be a father protecting his daughter." Therightmessages.com.
- "One of the first duties of a father is to protect his daughter from crying or else make those who make her cry to pay for their crimes." Therightmessages.com.
- "I may seem quiet and reserved but if you mess with my daughter, I will break out a level of crazy that will make your nightmares seem like a happy place." Pinterest.com.

I don't share these quotes to make you feel guilty. I share them to acknowledge that the guilt you feel about not being active in my life may be caused, in part, by feeling like you didn't protect me. When I was young, I don't remember ever feeling like I was missing out on having a father to protect me. Granted, that desire for fatherly protection is an inherent part of my longtime desire to be your little girl, but I wasn't left unprotected. God protected me beyond establishing boundaries.

When I was seventeen, Mom was married to her last husband. I came home from school and Mom asked me to go to Sears to pick up a rubber stamp for her husband's business. I went to Sears and picked up the stamp. Nothing seemed particularly dangerous about the errand. I arrived home safely and gave the stamp to Mom.

Some days later, I am not certain how many, I came home from school and Mom told me she had received a visit from two Bureau of Investigation officers. They explained that her husband, which by this time she had separated from, had contracted someone to kill her. He did so because he was involved with a married woman. The married woman took out a contract on her husband also. Insurance was likely part of the motivation, but at seventeen I kind of went into shock at the first statement, "There is a contract out on my life."

What does that have to do with an errand to pick up a rubber stamp? That was how the contracted killer was supposed to identify who Mom was. She was supposed to pick up the stamp. But, instead, she sent me. I was the identified subject of the contract.

Fortunately, Mom's husband apparently wasn't particularly knowledgeable about making such contracts. He contracted with two undercover Bureau of Investigation officers. They were at Sears and saw me pick up the stamp. They later informed Mom about the contract. I never saw her husband again.

This is an example of the type of protection people tend to think about when they claim God as their protector. They view His protection as preventing bad things from happening. The Bible is full of verses that speak of God as a protector of His children, such as 2 Thessalonians 3:3, which states, "But the Lord is faithful, and he will strengthen you and protect you from the evil one."[1] But preventing bad experiences isn't always how God protects.

There are a lot of hurtful things that happen to children. And I experienced things that are hard to view through the eyes of faith in a loving God. But, as Ben Cerullo writes, "When you see things through the eyes of faith, God always is bigger than your problems. Fear, anxiety, and hopelessness melt away in the light of His glory."[2]

I have found through life that God's protection is not always preventing bad things from happening. In Matthew 5:45, in what we commonly call the Sermon on the Mount, Jesus taught the crowds of people that good and bad happen to everyone, the just and the unjust alike.[3] Sometimes God chooses to take us out of harm's way, like He did for me when Mom sent me to Sears to pick up the rubber stamp. At other times He uses other methods to protect us.

Sometimes God allows the bad to happen but helps His children so there are no lasting effects. Or sometimes He works it out for the good of the person that was hurt. God sees from eternity to eternity. We see only the finite that is in front of us. He works everything out from His eternal vantage point even though we may not understand it.

When I consider a father's protection, I realize you could have only done so much to protect me. You could have set boundaries. You may have been able to keep me out of the street as a child. But you would not have been around during every situation in my life in order to protect me. You likely would not have been able to protect me from the most difficult things I experienced. But also, you would not have been able to help me through it with my faith intact, and you would not have been able to work all of the bad experiences into the beautiful life that my heavenly Father has orchestrated for me. So, there is no reason to feel guilty about not being with me in my childhood to protect me.

Before I close, I want to share my favorite father/daughter quote: "A father holds his daughter's hand for a short while, but he holds her heart forever." Explorepic.com. No, you weren't there during my childhood and I don't have any memories of walking hand in hand with you. But I cherish the one memory I have of you when I was about two. You were holding me and standing in an empty room with hardwood floors. Mom was standing across the room holding Randy in her arms. In my memory I can sense it was not a loving family moment. Nevertheless, I still cherish the memory because you were holding me close, protecting me from whatever was going on and loving me. I shared this memory with you many years ago. You explained that it was probably the day Mom left New York and returned to Kansas with Randy, leaving me with you. Despite the unhappy setting of my memory, I cherish the love I felt from you. I still dream of walking hand in hand with you, even as I continue to long to be "your little girl!"

From me, the one who always wanted to be "your little girl!"

Julie

Julie McGhghy

Misconception of God's Protection

What do you think about when you consider God's protection? I must admit that I have struggled with having faith in God's promise of protection. Why? Because I experienced things in my life that on the surface do not look like protection. I have come to terms with all of those experiences and can now see God's love and protection in them. Even so, God's protection is a hard thing to explain when someone experiences the unimaginable and wonders where God was during that time.

As I have dug into the Scripture to get a better idea of God's protection, I found I have had a major misconception about it. Based on many conversations I have had with people over the years, I am confident I am not alone in this misconception.

As I relayed to Dad my experience of going to Sears to pick up a rubber stamp, only to find out later that I had been identified as the subject of a contract for murder, I probably shocked you with such a story. But after you got over the shock, you likely praised God for His protection. Preventing something horrible from happening is exactly what we are looking for when we think of and pray for God's protection.

How many stories can you recall of people who were supposed to be at the World Trade Center on 9/11 when the terrorist attack occurred, but they had been delayed for some reason and that delay saved their lives? Some were delayed because they overslept. Some had car troubles. Some missed their usual train into the city. Some stayed home because they woke up feeling sick. Some had babysitter problems that day that kept them home. Some elected to run an errand, or they had a meeting before going into the office. The stories go on and on. When we heard about them then, and occasionally still hear about them now, many of the people involved express gratitude to God for His protection. We also thank God for His protection in these situations, because when we think of God's protection, we think only about God's preventing some terrible thing from happening.

But what about when God doesn't prevent the terrible thing from happening? What about people who were severely injured in an accident and will never recover one hundred percent? Or the children who experienced horrible child abuse? Or rape victims? Where was God's protection for them? As Dr. Coker explains, "The gospel, if it works at all, must work in the tough places and not only in the easy places."[4] Talking about God's protection, not as just a biblical promise but through practical application, often brings us into the tough places.

If we hold onto the misconception that God only protects by preventing the terrible thing from happening, then we often find ourselves in the tough places. But that is not what God promised.

God's protection comes from the promise that no person or experience can separate us from God. When speaking to the Jews about His followers, which He called His "sheep," Jesus explained "And I give unto them [His sheep] eternal life; and they shall never perish, neither shall any *man* pluck them out of my hand. My Father, which gave *them* me, is greater than all; and no *man* is able to pluck *them* out of my Father's hand. I and *my* Father are one."[5] The protection Jesus promised is that no man can take us out of relationship with God.

The apostle Paul expanded on that promise by proclaiming,

> Who shall separate us from the love of Christ? *shall* tribulation, or distress, or persecution, or famine, or nakedness, or peril, or sword? As it is written, For thy sake we are killed all the day long; we are accounted as sheep for the slaughter. Nay, in all these things we are more than conquerors through him that loved us. For I am persuaded, that neither death, nor life, nor angels, nor principalities, nor powers, nor things present, nor things to come, nor height, nor depth, nor any other creature, shall be able to separate us from the love of God, which is Christ Jesus our Lord."[6]

To Jesus's promise that no man shall take us out of relationship with God, Paul added experiences. Paul listed very difficult experiences and explained that these cannot separate us from God. Likewise, nothing we experience, no matter how difficult, unspeakable, or horrific, can separate us from God. This is God's protection; that no man or experience can separate us from Him.

Consider what Christ Himself and the early church experienced. Christ and many of His disciples, people who stood and heard Him proclaim the promise that no person can take them out of God's hand, were crucified. They were persecuted, imprisoned, separated from their families to serve as slaves or killed. Where was God's protection then? It was right where He proclaimed it to be. Those Christians who suffered such atrocities found God to be faithful; they received the promised eternal life.

But is eternal life all we can count on? Is that all Jesus's disciples counted on? No. There is so much more that is incorporated into God's protection than just the prevention of terrible things in our lives.

The Fullness of God's Protection

God's protection goes so much further than just the prevention of terrible experiences in our lives. His very presence in our lives is part of His protection. Moses encouraged the people of Israel before he died, exhorting them to avoid being afraid because God would be with them and would neither fail nor forsake them.[7] But God's presence didn't mean no one would be hurt or die. The people still had to war against the inhabitants of the Promised Land. They still experienced terrible things. But God's presence was with them.

It was God's presence that assured Israel they could withstand all they would face. God promised Israel He would strengthen and help them; He would hold them with His righteous right hand (the symbol of His power).[8]

The psalmist praised God for His presence in times of trouble, acknowledging that through His presence God is our refuge and strength.[9]

I love another promise God made to Israel through Isaiah, especially in view of experiences in my life both based on my own bad decisions and unspeakable experiences I had no control over. God promised Israel they would not be put to shame, and they would forget the shame of their youth.[10] God is so faithful with this! As Christians, we can trust Him to erase the guilt and shame of our pasts.

It is easy to think of the bad decisions we have made and understand why we would feel guilt and shame. Certainly, I felt guilt and shame for the circumstances of my first pregnancy, which, as I explained previously, was the product of a relationship after I had left my first husband. I had been a Christian since childhood and through my youth. I knew the second relationship was not one that would be pleasing to God. Yet I got involved with another man and became pregnant. Oh, the guilt and shame!

It's harder to understand why anyone, whether a child or an adult, would feel guilt and shame for experiences outside of his or her control. While there are many types of abuse, we frequently think of sexual abuse when considering children and adults who feel guilt and shame for something that is outside of their control.

Barbara Hughes explains, in an article entitled *"Where Was God? Spiritual Questions of Sexually Abused Children"* published by the Center for Children and Theology, why children who have been sexually abused feel a deep sense of moral shame.

> Most sexual abuse is perpetrated by someone of greater physical or emotional power than the child. For this reason it is natural for children to be afraid that the abuser will hurt them even more if they resist, or that rejection or abandonment may ensue. Often girls and boys are taught not to make a fuss and to acquiesce before those in authority. Although

the assaults can be gentle and from a trusted family member, because most of these children are forced to have sexual arousal, they believe that they themselves allowed or wanted the abuse and that it was therefore their fault. They usually emerge from their experiences with a deep sense of moral shame.[11]

Admittedly, prepubescent children have little or no understanding of sexuality. Yet, the children may experience sexual arousal. Ms. Hughes explains "all they know is that someone is doing something to or in their bodies—something that they know or sense is wrong—and that at the same time parts of their bodies are also feeling desire."[12] She continues describing the shame that results.

> The shame associated with childhood sexual abuse comes not only from the confusion of arousal with consent. By their invasive, hurtful, or physically violent actions, abusers shame the very sexuality of their victims. The child's sense of self is damaged or destroyed in part because the abuser has vanquished the child's will about her or his own most private bodily core.... It is the very life force and the sense of self that have been shamed and ravaged.[13]

The damage and destruction to the sense of self occurs in other types of abuse as well, leading abused children and adults alike to feel guilt and shame. Yet God's love enables us to forget the shame. And He will not put us to shame.

When my shame was caused by my own decisions, I returned to Him, repented and God forgave me. His unconditional love erased that sin from His sight and welcomed me back as His child. As I matured as a child of God, all of the shame and guilt of my bad decisions and of the wrongs that were forced upon me were replaced by love and acceptance. This removal of our shame is part of God's great protection.

Another way God protects us is by working all things together for our good.[14] The apostle Paul explained to the church in Colossae that the afflictions he suffered were worked together for the sake of the body of Christ, which is the church.[15] What good did Paul's suffering do for the church? His sufferings allowed Paul to encourage the Christians who were also suffering due to their belief in Jesus Christ. His sufferings helped him better know God and His power in order to explain such things to the Christians.[16] And as God helped Paul endure the sufferings, Paul was empowered to live for God and ultimately attain eternal life.[17]

I have seen God work in this way in my own life. When I taught youth Sunday School classes, I often developed close relationships with teenagers. Some of them endured the dysfunction of their families, which often resulted in separated or divorced parents. Because I experienced the same types of dysfunction in my family as I grew up, I could empathize with the kids and encourage them through those times. I could assure them they were not the cause of the dysfunction or the separation. I could show them how to find God in the midst of such pain, and that God loves them with an everlasting love.

I have come to believe people who have been hurt in devastating ways by other people tend to draw to them people who have suffered in similar ways. Somehow discussions turn to those experiences. When we have thoroughly processed the emotional impact and spiritual questions resulting from such experiences, and God has removed our shame, each of us is prepared to help others. God uses each of us who have survived the unspeakable to encourage and help others who are on the path of survival. Developing these relationships and being able to help others is very satisfying. This is all part of God's working all things together for good, even the unutterable.

At the risk of stating the obvious, the mere fact that I can share with you my experiences and what I have learned about God as my Father is an example of how He has worked together everything I experienced for my own good and for the good of other believers. Would I have chosen many of the experiences I endured growing up? No. But I am thankful for how God protected me with His presence, removed the shame of my own bad decisions and the experiences I had no control over, orchestrated this very satisfying life and enabled me to minister to and encourage others.

The Timing of God's Protection

We can learn a great deal from the psalmists and other writers of Scripture about the timing of God's protection. As relates to the time of trouble that we endure, God protects us before it, during it, after it and guides us regarding future trouble.

Before difficult times occur, consider praying as David did that God will keep you from the hands of the wicked and preserve you from violent people.[18]

During difficult times, the apostle Paul acknowledged the trouble and focused on the results of God's protection: troubled but not distressed; perplexed but not in despair; persecuted but not forsaken; cast down but not destroyed.[19] One psalmist acknowledged God as his refuge, strength and a very present help in the midst of the trouble.[20] He further proclaimed as a result of God's presence he would not fear regardless of the challenges he had to face.[21]

King David expressed his faith in God's protection during times of trouble. He proclaimed that God would revive and save him in the midst of the trouble.[22] He also prayed for God's deliverance and defense during the attacks from his enemies.[23]

God also protects us after the experiences. After one of King David's sons raped one of David's daughters and another son killed the rapist, David acknowledged God would rise up to help his family.[24] God protected him after the experiences. Although the consequences of the rape and David's neglect to discipline the rapist occurred, God's presence never left David. God continued to work things out for good. These horrible experiences did not sever David's relationship with God. God protected him.

When we struggle with oppression and afflictions after some horrible event in our lives, God will come to us to deliver us. This deliverance may include removing us from the situations that continue to cause the oppression and afflictions, providing His peace that passes all understanding or removing the shame we have carried unnecessarily. God will help us recover from the situation in the way that is best for each of us.

After I learned that I had been identified as the target of a contracted murder, God protected me by removing my mom's husband from our lives. But that was not always how God delivered me after horrible events. Sometimes during my youth, I had to stay in some inappropriate situations. All the while God used my grandmother to help me be active in the church youth group in order to build friendships that helped establish my faith. He gave me peace that surpassed my understanding and helped me mature into a productive adult.

When I married and built a family with a wonderful Christian man, God taught me how to parent my children through the example of my in-laws and through my formal education. God led me to Mid-America Nazarene College to prepare to teach mathematics in junior and senior high schools. Except for a six-week assignment as a substitute teacher, I never taught in schools. Yet through my studies to prepare to teach, I learned how to manage a classroom. I was able to apply those skills to managing my own home. This is one way God protected me, and my children, from the consequences of the dysfunction and inappropriate experiences I had growing up. Had He not guided me in that way, I am confident I would have passed the pain and cycle of dysfunction onto my children. But God!

As David proclaimed when King Saul was pursuing him, "Many *are* the afflictions of the righteous: but the Lord delivereth him out of them all."[25]

More of the Fullness of God's Protection

There is still more to God's protection than just the prevention of terrible experiences in our lives, His presence, His promise that we will forget our shame and how He works out all things for our good. To me, this last part of God's protection is a sign of complete healing from the horrible experiences many of us endured. In spite of everything we experience, regardless if it is due to our own decisions or things outside of our control, there will come a time when we will be able to rejoice again because we trust Him and love His name.[26]

I can remember when my healing, as opposed to my survival mechanisms, began. I was in my early thirties. Trisha was an active part of the youth group at our church and the youth group was sponsoring a get-together for the girls at our home. There were also a few other women supervising the event. As is often the case when ten to twenty teenage girls get together, some drama arose. I don't remember what occurred, but I remember some of the girls had very hurt feelings. As we sat in a circle and talked through the events and hurt feelings, God began showing me that I had built a wall around my emotions. I didn't feel pain. I didn't feel joy. I just kind of existed. Through those teenage girls who were feeling all kinds of emotions, I discovered how I had sheltered myself for so many years. In my mind I had an image of a brick wall I had erected all around myself. And God seemed to impress on me that the time was coming, with my permission, when He would tear down that wall brick by brick.

It took several years for the entire wall to be dismantled. In fact, I must admit that I still have a brick or two up to protect myself from certain people in my life. But with each brick that was knocked down, I felt more joy in my life. I became a person who laughs often, shares funny stories with friends and family and rejoices over the life God has given me. It was only after I could rejoice in Him that God began opening doors for me to minister to other people. And at some point, I began waking in the morning and declaring like the psalmist, "This *is* the day *which* the Lord hath made; [I] will rejoice and be glad in it."[27]

As God showed me each brick I had erected to protect myself, I was able to repent of each survival mechanism, which was a stronghold impairing my relationship with God. As I learned to pray without ceasing and give thanks in everything, I was also able to rejoice evermore as Paul had encouraged the Thessalonians.[28] God didn't restore my joy, because I don't know that I ever had true joy. But God gave me joy! And He will do the same for you as you let go of the survival mechanisms you employed to protect yourself from further hurt.

Contemplate How God Has Protected You

As I explained above, talking about God's protection has always been difficult for me. Why? Because I experienced things that no one would expect to happen if God had been protecting me. But I am thrilled to study the Word and learn how expansive God's protection is. I encourage you to reflect on your life.

- What experiences did you have that caused you to struggle to understand how God could let it happen to you? How did you cope with it and survive the pain?

- Consider some of your most difficult experiences and identify examples where God protected you in each of the ways listed below:
1. Preventing people or experiences from destroying your relationship with Him.

2. Strengthening and helping you endure difficult experiences through His presence.

3. Helping you forget your shame.

4. Working all things together for your good.

5. Enabling you to rejoice.

- If you still feel shame and guilt, or are not yet able to rejoice evermore, then fall at your Father's feet and ask Him to help you continue healing. Focus on taking God at His word. Make note cards of scriptures that promise His protection and those about trusting Him. Pray those scriptures and ask God to help you trust Him more. Cry out as the father of the demon-possessed boy did in Mark 9:24, "Lord, I believe; help thou mine unbelief."

Write these things down for further prayerful contemplation. Let God show you how He has fathered you as you read the next chapter about having a place of safety.

8

A Place of Safety:

God is a Refuge

Hey Dad, it's me!

Today I want to share with you one of my favorite worship songs. As a worship song it should make me think about God as I sing it. And it does, but it also makes me think about you.

Gateway Worship with Melissa Loose recorded a song titled "The More I Seek You."[1] It is sung as a prayer to God, personifying worship at His feet and leaning against His chest in order to feel His heartbeat. It presents a very intimate picture of a deeply loving relationship between God and His children. Some people have criticized the song because it tends to romanticize the relationship, which certainly isn't how I view it. Instead, I view it as a fatherly relationship.

So, why does this song make me think of you? Because when singing it, I envision being a little girl sitting on your lap, my head leaning against your chest and hearing your heartbeat. In that vision, I feel safe. I feel loved. I feel fathered.

I am not aware of any time in my life when I was able to sit on your lap. Yet I still dream of being your little girl, cuddled safely and lovingly on your lap, hearing your heartbeat, signifying that I know you so well I understand what makes you tick. I don't recall ever feeling that safe and loved. Even in my earliest memory of you, when you were holding me and standing in an empty room with hardwood floors, I feel loved but not safe. So, when I sing this worship song, I am thankful that God filled my need for love and safety. And as I have walked with Him for many years, I have become more acquainted with Him every day, understanding more and more what makes Him tick. God is my refuge, a place of safety.

In my last letter I explained God's protection, which is different from God's being my refuge. Protection is the process of keeping me safe, while a refuge is a safe place. God protected me from harm when I was identified as the subject of a contract for murder. He did so through a process of ensuring Mom's husband did not contract with an actual murderer. By contrast, a refuge is a safe place. I could run to God as my safe place when I learned about the contract for murder and my identification as the subject. God calmed me. God loved me. At God's feet and on His knee with my head against His chest, I could feel safe and loved.

Through the years God also showed me that He is my refuge and my safe place, even when I don't know I need to run to Him or can't run to Him because of traumatic occurrences. As long as I live a life close to Him, communicating with Him, worshipping Him, seeking Him, acknowledging Him in my life, when I don't even know that I am in danger or I can't run to Him because I am so traumatized, God places me in a safe place and puts His hand over me so harm cannot reach me. I realize He doesn't physically place me somewhere. And the kind of harm I am describing is not physical harm, but mental, emotional and spiritual harm. He is my safe place.

You don't need to feel guilty, Dad! God is and always has been my safe place. Running to your lap would never have been as safe as running to God's. God exceeded what you could have done for me even had you been an active part of my life.

From me, the one who always wanted to be "your little girl!"

Julie

Julie McGhghy

Refuge Versus Protection

As I explained to Dad in the letter above, "protection" is a process. In the previous chapter I explained the fullness of God's protection, which included the processes of preventing bad things from happening, being present with us at all times, preventing or removing our shame, working all things together for our good and enabling us to rejoice. God does all of these things for His children. We cannot do anything to merit His protection. And we need not do anything to receive His protection. If we are His children, He protects us. I am thankful for God's protection in my life.

I am also thankful that God is my refuge. A refuge is a place of safety, protection or shelter. Often in Scripture we see people doing something in order to take refuge and be safe. David often wrote psalms about taking refuge. Various versions of the Bible translate the original Greek and Hebrew as "trust" or "refuge." The King James Version often translates the terms to read "trust," while the Amplified Bible translates the terms to read "refuge." You can see this in Psalm 11:1. In the King James Version it reads, "In the Lord put I my trust." Yet in the Amplified Bible it reads, "In the Lord I take refuge [and put my trust]." (Brackets in the original.) Whether putting our trust in God or taking refuge in God, we take a step toward God and find safety, making an affirmative, voluntary action to benefit from God as our refuge.

When King David returned to Jerusalem after Absalom's death, he wrote a psalm encouraging all of them who had put their trust (KJV) or had taken refuge (AMP) in God to rejoice.[2] When King Saul was pursuing David, David penned Psalm 7 and proclaimed he himself puts his trust (KJV) or takes refuge (AMP) in God.[3] Yet David also acknowledged that God is a constant place of refuge. No action is required in order for God to be a refuge.

David expressed to the people his strong confidence in God by declaring "God is a refuge for us."[4] God is! Period. No action needed. God is our refuge! How could David be so confident? Because God had previously been

David's refuge.[5] As we trust and take refuge in God, our confidence also grows over time, and we learn God is our refuge; no action is necessary.

Taking Refuge in God

Many years ago, my husband and I moved our family to a new home. The front yard had a drainage ditch near the street. It was difficult to maintain the mowing of the ditch and it was a bit unsightly. The ditch continued on past our house into our neighbor's yard. So, Mike and our neighbor decided to place a drainpipe in the ditch, cover it with soil and plant grass. It looked very nice when it was done, but the task was not accomplished as smoothly as Mike would have liked. In fact, many things in Mike's life were quite challenging at that time, and his life just wasn't running as smoothly as he had become accustomed.

The day came for a truck load of soil to be delivered and for Mike to spread the soil over the pipe. Back then we were pretty young and frugal. Mike did not see any reason to rent equipment, such as a Bobcat, to spread the dirt. Instead, he was sure he could move the dirt by a wagon on a lawn mower and spread the dirt with a shovel.

Mike had worked hard from about sunup until approximately 3:00 in the afternoon. He was tired. The job was going more slowly than he expected, and an unexpected storm was moving in. If the dirt in the driveway got wet, it would be impossible for him to spread it into the ditch. Therefore, he was working furiously to get the job done. By furiously, I mean energetically, feverishly and desperately.

Well, it turned out that Mike was not able to work furiously enough. The storm hit. And it seemed to hit only our yard. Now, Mike was no longer working furiously, as in energetically, but furiously, as in angrily. I have never before or since seen Mike feel so targeted by God. He literally stood in the rain looking at the sky almost visibly and audibly speaking angrily to God.

Mike was convinced that God was putting every obstacle possible in his way. Mike was so mad that he would not, or possibly could not, come in out of the rain. Instead, he continued working feverishly in the rain until the storm blew over and he completed the job.

Just as God **is** our refuge like David expressed, our house was a refuge from the storm. But did our house provide Mike shelter when he was angrily working outside in the midst of a downpour? No, because Mike did not seek the shelter. He did not run into it despite knowing he had a shelter available to him. He did not make an affirmative, voluntary action to take advantage of it. Just like our home, God is a shelter. However, if we do not run into it, taking refuge in it, we do not benefit from it.

It is wonderful to know that God is our refuge and we can trust Him, run to Him, whenever we need to take shelter. But it actually gets much better than that.

God as a Constant Refuge

As David proclaimed in a number of psalms, God is our refuge. He is constant. No action is necessary for Him to be our refuge. Consider the dialogue between God and Moses in Exodus 33.

> And the Lord said [to Moses], "I will cause all my goodness to pass in front of you, and I will proclaim my name, the LORD, in your presence. I will have mercy on whom I will have mercy, and I will have compassion on whom I will have compassion. But," he said, "you cannot see my face, for no one may see me and live."

> Then the Lord said, "There is a place near me where you may stand on a rock. When my glory passes by, I will put you in a cleft in the rock and cover you with my hand until I have passed by. Then I will remove my hand and you will see my back; but my face must not be seen."[6]

In this passage of Scripture, God has asked Moses to lead His people. Moses asked God to teach him His ways so he might know God and find favor with Him. He asked God to show him His glory. God agreed to do so. But first, God had to protect Moses from God's glory. Imagine that! God's glory is so great that He must protect us from it!

So, did God require Moses to run into the cleft of the rock for protection? No. God merely extended an invitation to Moses to stand near Him. "There is a place near me where you may stand on a rock."[7] If Moses chose to stand near God, then God would put him in the cleft of the rock and would be a refuge to Moses by placing His hand over him while God passed by him.

How does Moses's experience compare to Mike's experience? Mike did not experience God as his refuge while standing in the pouring rain. Why? Because Mike was not standing near God. Instead, Mike was angry at God. He was blaming God for sending all of the trials that were making life rather challenging at the time, even down to the miniscule detail of sending a storm that appeared only over our yard right at the time that Mike was trying desperately to complete a project. Mike was not standing near God.

Mike's experience is an example where an affirmative, voluntary action was required to benefit from God as his refuge. If we are not living close to God, standing near Him, responding willingly to God's invitations to draw near to Him, then we will not experience God's refuge without taking an affirmative, voluntary action first. In Mike's situation, he would have had to change his attitude, draw near to God and take refuge in Him.

God Is and Was My Constant Refuge

God showed me what it means that He is my refuge...a constant, no action required refuge. I had not been looking for God as my refuge. I didn't even know I would need Him to be a refuge for me. But I found myself in a situation I wasn't prepared for, had never considered would happen and surprised me by how it turned out. I was so surprised that I asked God to show me what had just happened.

In previous chapters I mentioned that I have experienced things in my life, in my childhood, that are hard to view through the eyes of faith in a loving God. Likewise, such experiences are hard to view through the promise of God's protection. For so many years these experiences caused me to struggle with understanding God's protection. In fact, I didn't understand it until I researched it in preparation for writing this book.

Divorce was prevalent in my family, not only my immediate family as I grew up but also in my extended family. My mom, aunts and uncles were all married multiple times. With each marriage new people were added to the family, people who were not blood relatives. These people may be step-parents, step-siblings, step-grandparents, step-aunts and step-uncles. So, I was exposed to far too many "family members" for me to account for. And I found myself left alone with some of these "family members." A number of them, all at different times, treated me inappropriately.

God protected me from the vast majority of the negative impact of such actions. Although I never told anyone about any of the situations, I saw the individuals were removed from my life over time. I never, however. forgot the experiences. Thankfully, I didn't have to face the individuals or be concerned about continued violation from any of them.

But that changed not too many years ago. Totally unexpectedly I found myself face-to-face with one of the men who had violated me as a child. By that time, I was a mature adult. I had independent decision-making authority and capacity. I could choose how I would handle the situation. Because other people were involved and would have been affected by my decision, I chose to spend some time with him.

I hadn't seen this person for thirty or more years. During that time, I had laid the issue on the altar many times. And eventually I successfully left it there at Jesus's feet. I believed in my heart that I had dealt with the abuse.

I didn't harbor any bitterness or unforgiveness. However, I never had to test that belief because I never had to have contact with the man.

While I was visiting someone close to me for several weeks, I encountered the man occasionally visiting the home I was staying in because he was helping my host handle certain difficulties in her life. When he invited my host, her family and me to visit his home and then go out for dinner with him and his wife, I accepted the invitation. At the end of that evening, I hugged him and thanked him for dinner and the time we had just shared.

How could that be? How could I have hugged him and been sincerely grateful for time spent with him again? I had to ask myself and God these very questions. It isn't by my own strength, determination or even denial! It is only by God's healing touch that I was able to face the man after so many years.

That evening I was able to see the man with no bitterness, hate or unforgiveness arising within me. My body did not start shaking like it used to do when I merely spoke about him. I was able to look him in the eye, have a conversation and enjoy the evening.

Don't get me wrong, I did not invite him to be part of my life on an ongoing basis. I haven't seen or spoken to the man again since that evening. I don't need or want him in my life. But that evening proved to me that I can be calm and cordial when social circumstances find him and me in the same room.

God is my refuge. He was my refuge when I was a child, and He protected me from the abuse. Yes, the abuse occurred. But, no, the abuse did not destroy me!

After returning home from my visit, I began seeking God about the whole issue. I still needed to make sure that I had healed from the abuse and forgiven the man. I needed to know I was not merely walking around in denial. God directed me to the passages regarding His being my refuge. I learned that I needed to take refuge in Him in order to receive His protection. I was standing on solid scriptural grounds with that belief. Yet I couldn't understand how God was my refuge when I was a child and did not know to run to Him, or, when I could not run to Him due to the mere shock, shame and embarrassment of the situation. If I did not run to Him, how then was He my refuge?

I was still struggling with such questions when Mike and I took a cruise to Alaska. One of the excursions we took in Alaska was rock climbing and rappelling. As I was climbing a sixty-foot rock wall, I was kept safe by a guy who was holding my ropes to keep me from falling. He encouraged me and guided me when I could not find what seemed to me to be a secure foothold. During one such time, the guy yelled at me, "Use that cleft, the cleft in the rock."

Immediately, my heart began singing, "He hideth my soul in the cleft of the rock that shadows a dry, thirsty land. He hideth my life in the depths of His love and covers me there with His hand, and covers me there with His hand."[8]

From that moment until I got home from vacation and had an opportunity to research the "cleft of the rock," I knew the key to God's being my refuge when I did not know to run to Him. When I could not run to Him, I was hidden by Him in the cleft of the rock. That is when I found, as Paul Harvey would say, the "rest of the story." That is when I found the beauty of God as my refuge.

You see, as long as I am standing near God as He has invited me to do, then I need not take affirmative, voluntary action to obtain refuge from Him. Instead, when I stand near Him, where He has invited me to stand, He puts me in the cleft of the rock and He covers me with His hand to protect me. Through all of these years, God has been my refuge and He has protected me from the effects of the abuse.

But wait, there is more! Remember in Exodus 33:23, God told Moses that after He had passed by God would remove His hand, and Moses would see His back.[9] Because God is not a physical being, God is not referring to

His physical back. Instead, God is referring to the after-effects of His radiant glory.

God is and was my refuge. He placed me in the cleft of the rock for my protection. As I was climbing the rock in Alaska, I beheld the after-effects of His glorious refuge and protection, for God removed His hand. God even gave me an opportunity to confirm that I had effectively placed the abuse on the altar and I am healed. He removed my shame many years ago. He worked it all together for good. I can now help others who have had similar experiences or other types of abuse to see how God has protected them and how He is and was their refuge. And I can rejoice in the Lord. He is my savior, protector and refuge!

Forgiveness – A Refuge from Sin

God is a refuge for His children. I personally believe He is a refuge for all children or others who lack the capacity to choose between His ways or the world's ways. Once you have acquired that capacity, He becomes your refuge when you enter into a relationship with Him through salvation. As explained above, there are two ways to be protected by the refuge he offers you: 1) Take an affirmative, voluntary action to take shelter in Him; or 2) Stand so near Him, where He has invited you, so He can be your refuge even when you are not able to take the affirmative, voluntary action to seek His shelter.

We learn so much from David, a man after God's own heart,[10] about how to draw near to God to be protected from danger whenever it arises in our lives. First, we must live a life of trusting God and pouring out our hearts to Him.[11] Pouring out our heart to God means we openly communicate with Him at all times, not just when we need Him. We can pour out our hearts to God no matter the emotional state we are in: in praise and worship; in brokenness; in confusion; in elation. When we trust God, we need not hide our feelings. We need only be real with Him.

David and other psalmists teach us to call on the Lord.[12] The Lord wants to commune with us. He waits to hear from us.[13] Because we live in the world, which is limited in time and space, we often find ourselves restrained from calling on Him. Men began calling on the Lord from the third generation of life.[14] And God still wants to hear from us regularly. We can call on Him in praise, worship, thanksgiving, trouble, heartbreak and repentance.[15] God just wants to hear from us!

It is interesting that calling upon the Lord is associated with righteousness, while not calling upon the Lord is associated with wickedness. David proclaimed, "The eyes of the Lord *are* upon the righteous, and his ears *are open* unto their cry... *The righteous* cry, and the Lord heareth, and delivereth them out of all their troubles."[16] When the apostle Paul wrote to his son in the faith, Timothy, he admonished Timothy to flee from youthful lusts, "but follow righteousness...with them that call on the Lord out of a pure heart."[17]

On the other hand, not crying out to the Lord is part of wickedness. King David acknowledged that "workers of iniquity" do not call on the Lord.[18] While lamenting over Jerusalem, the psalmist Asaph prayed God would pour out His wrath upon the "heathen" and the kingdoms that have not called upon His name.[19] People who live outside of God's ways and His will do not call upon Him.

Calling on the Lord is part of a close, intimate relationship with God, answering His invitation to a close walk with Him, just as Moses did. In that relationship we do not have to take an affirmative, voluntary step toward God when we face troubles. Instead, we will already be close enough for Him to protect us by placing His hand over us until the time He shows us the after-effects of His glory.

It is also important to note the relationship between "refuge" and sin. BibleMesh reminds us we live in a world of sin, which wreaks havoc on our lives, creating threats to our physical, spiritual and emotional wellbeing.[20] Yet, as our refuge, God saves us from sin and all its consequences.[21]

The Lord is our refuge in the Day of Judgment. Though He will bring a day of reckoning for sin, He grants His people forgiveness and gives them refuge from His wrath (Nahum 1:7; Deuteronomy 32:37). Indeed, the greatest need of all men and women is shelter from the horrible consequences of sin, and this word in Scripture reminds us that God offers such shelter.[22]

The sacrifices of the Old Testament, which only covered sin and had to be repeated regularly, were not sufficient to be a refuge that takes away sin.[23] But, thankfully, God provides us refuge from sin through the blood of Jesus Christ.[24] Even more, we are freed from the dominion of sin and live under grace.[25] We are now servants of righteousness.[26]

When sin still had dominion over us, we often felt guilt and shame, because the fruit of unrighteousness includes shame.[27] We even felt shame for things that were not of our choice or doing. Yet when we live under God's refuge, we are freed from shame! The fruit we now bear is holiness and everlasting life.[28]

What a great refuge our God is, and I want to remain so close to Him that He puts me in the cleft of the rock and places His hand over me for protection. And what a glorious day it is when He removes that hand and shows me the after-effect of His glory! Hallelujah!

Contemplate How God Has Been Your Refuge

I am so thankful that in addition to God's protecting us, He is also a place of safety. What an experience it was when I learned that He had placed me in a cleft of the rock with His hand over me until I was able to see how He was glorified in the difficult and abusive experiences of my past.

Now I encourage you to reflect on your own life.

- Did you have experiences that are hard to view from the eyes of faith?

- Did you run to God for protection?

- Were you close enough to God at that time that He placed you in a cleft of the rock without your having to move toward Him, or did you take steps toward Him in order to find safety?

- If you can now see the after-effects of God's glory in those situations, spend some time thanking God for showing you His glory. If you have not yet been able to identify His glory in the situations, ask God to show you. Keep a record of what you learn from God.

_____

_____

_____

_____

_____

_____

Write these things down for further prayerful contemplation. Let God show you how He has fathered you as you read the next chapter about being more than a statistic.

9

By the Numbers:

We are More Than a Statistic

Hey Dad, it's me!

I've been thinking lately about why you may feel guilty about leaving Randy and me when we were young and your not being part of our lives as we grew up. I remember overhearing a conversation once when I had visited your home. I was probably in my mid-thirties at the time. Someone in your family commented to someone else, I don't remember who, that they felt sorry for Randy and me because we grew up without our father. That comment shocked me because I didn't view my life as being pitiable, especially by someone who really didn't know much about my life.

Now that I've given much thought to the guilt you have felt, I wonder if it is driven in part by the many statistics about children raised without an active father in their lives. I will admit, when focusing on the statistics, life looks pretty dismal. But what I've come to learn, Dad, is that I am more than a statistic!

Did I fall into some of the traps that many girls raised without an active father in their lives fall into? Yes. But did that define me? No.

One thing I've learned about my heavenly Father is that He doesn't care much for categorizing people into numbers. When God instructed Moses to take a census after he brought the children of Israel out of Egypt, He did so in order to establish the offerings of the people for operating and maintaining the tabernacle.[1] Because this census was for the benefit of maintaining worship, it actually benefitted the people and did not separate them into harmful categories.

Later, King David ordered a census of the people of Israel.[2] The results of the census were reported only for the fighting men. The Bible is not clear why, but God was angry at David for conducting the census, and He punished the people for it. Those who write about David's census commonly point to his motives for taking the census as the reason God was angry. Some speculate David's intention was purely self-aggrandizement by quantifying his power.[3] Others assume David's intent was to increase the power of his kingdom as opposed to remaining humbly reliant upon God.[4] Another reason proposed is that David no longer trusted God for safety and sought comfort in the military power of his nation.[5] From my perspective, David categorized the people in order to treat them differently from the general population, and he had different expectations for them. Numbering and categorizing people for different treatment does not please God.

The apostle Paul explained to the Christians in the churches of Galatia that there are no different categories among believers, neither Jew nor Greek, bond nor free, male nor female.[6] We are all children of God...period. God has no use for numbering and assigning people into harmful categories. Our life experiences do not define us; our relationship with God does.

Dad, you need not feel guilty based on the number of overwhelming and dismal statistics about children raised without a father in the home, or any other statistic for that matter. I was fathered by the best, my heavenly Father. And He has far exceeded anything I could have ever dreamed for my life.

From me, the one who always wanted to be "your little girl!"

Julie McGhghy

Statistics Can Be Overwhelming

As a child I didn't pay much attention to statistics, but in my first year of college, I took sociology and psychology classes. Both were filled with statistics about a number of different categories people fall into. I obtained a bachelor of arts degree in mathematics in order to teach secondary math. Part of the required curriculum was a class called Probability and Statistics. In the class I learned how to read statistical information and how to properly structure a statistical study. The more I learned about statistics, the more I realized how much statistics play into people's perspective on life.

As I grew older and began paying attention to political activities, I realized how statistics drive governmental and social policy. That's when I began feeling like I was just a statistic; and I realized I wasn't supposed to be able to accomplish much of anything. Yes, I did make choices that were consistent with what some of the statistics said I would make since I was raised without my biological father active in my life. But, as I told Dad in my letter above, those decisions and the statistics did not define me. And your decisions and the statistics don't define you.

Life by Statistics

It is important to understand the impact of fatherlessness in our world whether or not we define our lives by the statistical categories we do or do not fall into. Statistics help us understand that and are important for developing governmental policy and social programs. But we must avoid focusing on them, applying them to our own lives and allowing them to create a self-fulfilling prophecy for us. In this section I will share some of the statistics. Even if you have little or no appreciation for statistics, or never considered yourself just a statistic, I encourage you to continue reading this section to get an idea of the obstacles faced by people raised with an absent father. In the next section, we will view ourselves through God's eyes!

Admittedly, fatherlessness is an issue worldwide. However, the following statistics are based only on American homes. More than 24.7 million children live in a home without their biological father present.[7] Some advocates for fathering assert "almost every social ill faced by America's children is related to fatherlessness."[8] Below is a list of statistics describing the impact fatherlessness has on children in America.

- "Children in father-absent homes are almost four times more likely to be poor. In 2011, 12 percent of children in married-couple families were living in poverty, compared to 44 percent of children in mother-only families."[9]
- "Children living in female-headed families with no spouse present had a poverty rate of 47.6 percent, over 4 times the rate in married-couple families."[10]
- "The U.S. Department of Health and Human Services states, 'Fatherless children are at a dramatically greater risk of drug and alcohol abuse.'"[11]
- "Children of single-parent homes are more than twice as likely to commit suicide."[12]
- "Diminished self-concept, and compromised physical and emotional security (children consistently report feeling abandoned when their fathers are not involved in their lives, struggling with their emotions and episodic bouts of self-loathing)"[13]
- "Behavioral problems (fatherless children have more difficulties with social adjustment, and are more likely to report problems with friendships, and manifest behavior problems; many develop a swaggering, intimidating persona in an attempt to disguise their underlying fears, resentments, anxieties and unhappiness)"[14]
- "Truancy and poor academic performance (71 percent of high school dropouts are fatherless; fatherless children have more trouble

academically, scoring poorly on tests of reading, mathematics, and thinking skills; children from father absent homes are more likely to play truant from school, more likely to be excluded from school, more likely to leave school at age 16, and less likely to attain academic and professional qualifications in adulthood)"[15]

- "Delinquency and youth crime, including violent crime (85 percent of youth in prison have an absent father; fatherless children are more likely to offend and go to jail as adults)"[16]
- "Promiscuity and teen pregnancy (fatherless children are more likely to experience problems with sexual health, including a greater likelihood of having intercourse before the age of 16, foregoing contraception during first intercourse, becoming teenage parents, and contracting sexually transmitted infection; girls manifest an object hunger for males, and in experiencing the emotional loss of their fathers egocentrically as a rejection of them, become susceptible to exploitation by adult men)"[17]
- "Life chances (as adults, fatherless children are more likely to experience unemployment, have low incomes, remain on social assistance, and experience homelessness)"[18]
- "Future relationships (father absent children tend to enter partnerships earlier, are more likely to divorce or dissolve their cohabiting unions, and are more likely to have children outside marriage or outside any partnership)"[19]

The above statistics are limited to the impact on children growing up without an active father in the home. Many of these children will also suffer child abuse[20] and child sexual abuse.[21] Abused children often experience mental health disorders, addictions and other issues related to child abuse, including "risk for intimate partner violence, alcoholism and alcohol abuse, illicit drug abuse, smoking and drinking at an early age, depression, and suicide attempts."[22] Child sexual abuse victims "are at significantly greater risk for later posttraumatic stress and other anxiety symptoms, depression and suicide attempts."[23] Psychological problems often "lead to significant disruptions in normal development and often have a lasting impact, leading to dysfunction and distress well into adulthood."[24]

If we focus on these statistics, we can easily view ourselves as just a statistic, especially when one or more of the statistics prove to be true in our lives. In my childhood, I experienced periods of poverty, living in subsidized housing and being on the welfare rolls. I definitely performed under my academic potential. I graduated from high school with a "C" average, yet as an adult I graduated magna cum laude with a bachelor's degree and cum laude with a juris doctorate. I experienced a teenage pregnancy, although I was twenty when she was born.

My early adulthood was a bit traumatic, having married at eighteen and separated at nineteen, having a child at twenty, and remarrying at twenty-one. Until I was twenty-one, my life looked like one statistic after another. But that isn't the end of the story. And that isn't my identity.

Life Change

So what happened when I was twenty-one that made the difference in my life? I finally became very serious about my relationship with God. Even though I considered myself a Christian after I was baptized as a child, and I was very active in my church and youth group during high school, I wasn't dedicated to really knowing God and learning His ways until after I had my daughter. As I learned more about God and His ways, I began learning that I was much more than a statistic. And God began helping me make better decisions. He taught me how to be a wife and mother.

As I explained to Dad in a previous letter, God began showing me His everlasting love one day as I was living deep in sin. I was in a relationship I should not have been in and I was pregnant. Then one afternoon while I was all alone in my bedroom, I reached for the Bible. And there He was, assuring me with His Word again, drawing me back to Him. No, I didn't make any immediate changes in my life that afternoon, yet I knew God was drawing me and I would eventually return to Him. And I did.

When I was about three months pregnant, I had returned to my hometown and lived with my mom. I moved back home because Trisha's biological father and I did not have the means to care for this precious baby and support ourselves.

At my mom's home, I shared a small bedroom with my infant daughter. As I was awake one night feeding her, I knew I had to return to God, because I could not raise Trisha without His help. I pulled out my Bible again and asked God to show me He is real! I had convinced myself that He couldn't be real because He wouldn't have let me mess up my life so badly if He were. But God loves us enough to allow us to make choices. And I made some bad ones.

God forgave me. I wrote to Trisha's father and explained I would be raising Trisha alone, because I needed to raise her in a Christian home. I started attending church again, just Trisha and me. That was difficult because people who knew me as part of the youth group had a difficult time accepting me as a single mother. I couldn't get away from the guilt and shame. Then God moved me to a different church where people didn't know my prior life. They obviously knew I was a single mom with a very young baby. But they just wanted to show me God's love. And they did.

God was moving in my life in ways I could not have dreamed of. When Trisha was six months old, I began dating a young man I worked with at a small airport. Even that was God orchestrated.

When I first moved back to my hometown, I had to find a job. I called for an interview for a position at the Johnson County Industrial Airport. When I scheduled the interview, the scheduler asked if I knew where the airport was. Sure, I knew. I had lived in that town almost all of my life. So, I explained that I knew where it was and would not need directions.

The day on which the interview was scheduled, I drove to the airport. I explained to the desk clerk I was there for an interview. She informed someone and took me back to meet with one of the owners of the business at the airport. I was offered the job that very afternoon and started working the next day. It wasn't until sometime later that I realized I had gone to the wrong airport for the interview. I drove to the Johnson County Executive Airport, not the Johnson County Industrial Airport. I didn't have an appointment for an interview at the Executive Airport. I didn't even know they had a job opening. But God did! And He led me to that airport at a time when one of the owners was available to interview me and offer me a job. It was at that job I met Mike, the young man I later began dating and eventually married.

As I mentioned in an earlier chapter, it wasn't long after Trisha was born that she became very sick. She struggled with respiratory issues. Doctors were not able to diagnose the issues. A cycle of hospitalizations began. Each time she was so sick she could hardly breathe, Trisha's doctors would admit her into the hospital. She would stay under an oxygen tent for about two weeks until her lungs cleared up. Then I would take her home and her health would start declining again. It would be about two weeks before the doctors would put her back into the hospital under an oxygen tent. Our life had become a cycle of two weeks in the hospital, then two weeks out of the hospital. This lasted until she was thirteen months old.

In order to afford Trisha's medicines and medical bills, I had to work two jobs. I found a full-time job at a telecommunication supply company. The job paid better than the airport and I worked there Monday through Friday. I continued working at the airport during the evenings.

During the two weeks Trisha was in the hospital, I would wake up at 5:00 a.m., drive to the hospital to visit Trisha on my way to my full-time job and return to the hospital during my lunch hour. After my day was over at the telecommunication supply company, I would go back to the hospital for a few minutes and then drive to the airport for my evening job, working until 9:00. After 9:00 I went back to the hospital to visit Trisha until about 10:00 or so. I then drove home to get some sleep before starting the routine again the next day.

These were hard times but God was with us. Remember Mike? One day when I visited the hospital during my lunch hour, I found Mike sitting in Trisha's room with her. I had never asked him to visit her. He never mentioned he was going to. He just did it. At that time Mike was in his junior year at a college located only three blocks from the hospital. Between his classes he went to the hospital and sat with Trisha. Who wouldn't fall in love with such a man? I have always teased him by saying he fell in love with Trisha and married me because we were a package deal!

God far exceeded anything I would have ever dreamed when He orchestrated Mike and me meeting at a job I was never planning to interview for! He did so just as the apostle Paul described Him to the church in Ephesus: "Now unto him that is able to do exceeding abundantly above all that we ask or think, according to the power that worketh in us."[25] And He continues exceeding my every dream as Mike and I walk through our lives together. And through the years, God has shown me I am not just a statistic!

More Than a Statistic

We are so much more to God than a mere statistic, no matter what our life experience has been. God does not see us as other people do; He looks at our hearts.[26] He knows us better than anyone else, even better than we know ourselves.[27] And He loves us, even before we experience salvation.

As King David proclaimed, each of us is "fearfully and wonderfully made."[28] When we were formed in our mother's womb, before we ever considered salvation, we were fearfully and wonderfully made. This means God formed us in a way that is unique among His creation and that inspires awe and reverence for Him.[29] He made each of us for a particular purpose.[30] And in His great love, He chose us to stand holy and blameless before Him.[31] This is how He made us and why He draws us to salvation, into a relationship with Him, so that when we are saved, He rejoices over us with joy.[32] The Amplified Bible paints a beautiful picture in Zephaniah 3:17.

> The Lord your God is in the midst of you, a Mighty One, a Savior [Who saves]! He will rejoice over you with joy; He will rest [in silent satisfaction] *and* in His love He will be silent *and* make no mention [of past sins, or even recall them]; He will exult over you with singing.[33]

Isn't this a beautiful picture of God as we come to salvation, entering into the relationship He has always sought with us after the perfect relationship He created with man was destroyed by the sin of Adam and Eve? Can't you just envision Him in the bodily form of Christ, standing and raising His hands in excitement that you have turned your back on your past and on the world and reached up to Him as your Savior and Father?

For me, I even see myself sitting on His knee as a child, with my head against His chest, listening to his very heartbeat, knowing I am His child and I am loved. At that moment of salvation, when God has reconciled us to Him, in God's sight we are a new creation; nothing we have done previously exists and everything is new.[34] This is how God sees us and this is who we are.

Who We Are in Christ

At the point of salvation, the moment you become a child of God, statistics no longer apply to you! The world no longer knows you, just as it did not know Jesus Christ.[35] You are no longer merely born of blood or by the will of your parents, but you are born of God.³⁶ You are chosen by God to be His child.³⁷ There are no studies, no statistics, that can describe a child of God!

You are a child of God because God has drawn you to Himself.³⁸ You are now forgiven and cleansed of your past.³⁹ And because of that cleansing, you are not subject to condemnation from God.⁴⁰

As you mature as a child of God, you will be shown the things that please Him. As I described in a previous chapter, while I trained for long distance cycling, God began blessing me with opportunities to view His creation and wildlife. I rejoiced with God every time I saw something, like the peacock near a country road. The more I rejoiced in Him for the sightings, the more opportunities He provided for me to view His creation. He showed me the earth is His footstool,⁴¹ so when I love, appreciate and am thankful for nature (His creation), I am worshiping at His feet. You too will grow in the knowledge of what is pleasing to God. And you will want to do more of the things that please Him, leaving less time to do things that do not.

As expected, your life will become much richer as you seek to please God. However, often old friends or family who do not share the same relationship with God will not understand. This can sometimes cause strife in your relationships. But do not be concerned or afraid. As a child of God, you will be able to handle the strife. Just like the apostle Paul, you will be able to do all things, endure all strife and difficult circumstances through Christ who will strengthen you.⁴²

It is also important to remember that a relationship with God does not eliminate all hurtful and challenging situations in life. I certainly experienced challenges while I was a Christian, the most difficult being my seven-year-old son's plan to kill himself. Yet God walked with Mike and me through that, giving us wisdom and strength. As I explained in a previous chapter, Jesus taught that good and bad happen to everyone, the just and the unjust alike.⁴³ We do not escape the difficulties of this world simply because we walk in relationship with God.

The apostle Paul challenged the church in Rome, asking what experiences could separate us from the love of Christ.[44] He listed some pretty extreme difficulties in life, such as tribulation, distress, persecution, famine, nakedness, peril or the sword.[45] In response to his own question, Paul boldly proclaimed, "Nay, in all these things we are more than conquerors through him that loved us."[46] You will likely never experience these same extreme difficulties in your own life, but you will experience difficulties. And some of them may be extreme. But you can have the same confidence as the apostle Paul. You, too, are more than a conqueror through Christ who loves you.

Above everything else, who we are in Christ includes being the temple of God and a member of a royal priesthood. We are God's temple because His precious Holy Spirit lives within us.[47] Right there within you, you have access to the greatest teacher! The Holy Spirit will teach you all things you need to know about a life with Christ and remind you all Christ taught here on earth.[48] The Holy Spirit will reveal to you the deep things of God.[49] I have found as I have learned more and more about God that I have grown to love Him more and more as well. And I don't claim to know much! But I know more and love Him more than I did when I started walking with Him. I am confident the same will happen for you as you let the Holy Spirit teach and guide you.

And, finally, you are a member of a royal priesthood.[50] What does that mean? It means you have been given access to the throne room of God and can stand in His very presence.[51] You can come to Him boldly.[52] You can freely offer sacrifices of praise, thanksgiving and worship. You can also feel free to share your heart, your hurts, your questions, your joy, your dreams, your love. You can be you at the feet of Jesus!

Contemplate How God Has Made You More Than a Statistic

Have you ever felt like just a statistic? Even as you read this chapter, did you see yourself in the statistics? If so, which ones?

_____
_____
_____
_____
_____

I don't want you to focus on the statistics. Instead, I encourage you to really consider who you are in Christ.

- Do you relate to that desire to sit at Jesus's feet, or on His knee with your head against His chest, hearing His heartbeat? How have you encountered such intimacy with God?

_____
_____
_____
_____
_____

- As a chosen, forgiven, cleansed child of God, are you living free from condemnation? If not, consider some of the scriptures referred to in this chapter and listed in the Notes and replace your thoughts of condemnation with God's assurance.

- Consider an example of how God has helped you through the difficulties of life since you've been a Christian.

- Are you as confident as the apostle Paul that no experience in life can separate you from God? If not, review the scriptures referred to in this chapter and listed in the Notes and pray them to build your confidence.

- Spend some time thanking God for His goodness, sharing with Him your praise, joys, and, if any still linger, your hurts and questions. Be yourself before the Lord. Rest on His knee with your head on His chest and hear His heartbeat for you!

_____

_____

_____

_____

_____

_____

Write the above responses down for further prayerful contemplation. Let God show you how He has fathered you as you read the next chapter about who you see in the mirror.

10

Self-Image:

What Do You See in the Mirror?

Hey Dad, it's me!

Since I established in my last letter that I am more than a statistic, I have realized you may feel guilty because you feel I have a poor self-image due to your absence in my life. As I think about my early visits with you, I can understand why you might think that. When I first met you when I was sixteen, you would have been right, which was likely evident when I really didn't have much to say to you during our visit.

I have learned through the years that self-image incorporates more than just what one sees when looking in the mirror. It also includes how a person views her own performance and her relationships.

Like most teenage girls, I was never very happy with what I saw when I looked in the mirror. I had big ears, big feet and was tall. I didn't date too many boys, leading me to believe I wasn't very attractive.

I viewed myself as of average intelligence, which is what my grades revealed. I didn't feel like I had anything particularly interesting to say to people so I didn't talk much. And despite Grandma's efforts to provide me with voice lessons, I was not particularly talented.

I had friends, but they weren't close friendships. None of them proved to be life-long relationships or even lasted until the end of high school. I would develop friendships, but then we would all move on to other things and other people.

The only close relationship I had at that time was with Grandma. Oh, how she loved me. And I loved her. And she was always interested in what I had to say. She thought I was beautiful, intelligent and talented. We spent many Saturday nights together watching Lawrence Welk and CHiPS. I dreamed of being beautiful like the women on Lawrence Welk and dancing across the ballroom floor with the most handsome man there, which was Tom Netherton in Grandma's and my opinions. He was tall, blond, blue-eyed, and could sing like no one else. Afterwards we would watch CHiPs, and I would swoon over Erik Estrada who played "Ponch." He was not tall but had the dark features of his parents of Puerto Rican decent. Apparently, Grandma and I could find beauty in tall, short, dark or light. It didn't matter as long as they were talented.

Thankfully, a person's self-image changes over time based on the person's experience and relationships. I recently read an article on my.clevelandclinic.org explaining "how we think about ourselves affects how we feel about ourselves and how we interact with others in the world around us."[1] As I think back on how I thought of myself when we first met, it is no wonder I had few friends who stayed around for any time at all. I didn't feel like I had much to offer, and that seemed to reflect in how others viewed me as well.

Grandma's opinions of me were quite positive, and she was always generous with her praise. It was through her eyes that I first started seeing how God views me. I had grown accustomed to people comparing me to others, such as my beautiful cousins, and me falling short. But through Grandma's eyes and God's teaching, I learned comparisons among people was not an appropriate standard for assessing oneself. The apostle Paul made it clear in 2 Corinthians 10:12 and 18 that comparing ourselves to other people was not wise. Instead, it is only God's commendation that matters.

In order to acquire a consistent self-image, it is important to have a consistent standard to measure oneself by. Other people's appearances, performances and relationships are not consistent, providing an ever-changing standard of measurement. The only constant measure available is God. He never changes. According to Hebrews 13:8, He is the same yesterday, today and forever.² It is through His eyes that I now view myself.

The apostle Paul started many churches, wrote two-thirds of the New Testament and suffered greatly for the cause of Christ. Admirably, he understood it was only by the grace of God that he accomplished anything. As he explained in 1 Corinthians 15:10, "But by the grace of God I am what I am: and his grace which *was bestowed* upon me was not in vain: but I laboured more abundantly than they all: yet not I, but the grace of God which was with me."

I am glad that over time my self-image improved, not because of my experiences and accomplishments, but because I learned to apply the consistent standard of God's assessment of me. Through Him I view myself as loved, beautiful, talented, and marvelously and wonderfully made! He helped me develop a positive self-image in spite of the comparisons others made or the fact that you weren't here to help me along the way. There is no reason for you to feel guilty. God developed in me the self-image that delights Him.

From me, the one who always wanted to be "your little girl!"

What Do You See in the Mirror?

So many of us look in the mirror and pick ourselves apart based on how we look. Yet our self-image includes so much more and has been developed over a lifetime.

Self-image is the personal view, or mental picture, that we have of ourselves. Self-image is an "internal dictionary" that describes the characteristics of the self, including such things as intelligent, beautiful, ugly, talented, selfish, and kind. These characteristics form a collective representation of our assets (strengths) and liabilities (weaknesses) as we see them.[3]

If you recognize and own your assets and potentials while being realistic about your liabilities and limitations, you have a positive self-image.[4] You gain confidence in your thoughts and actions when you have a positive self-image.[5] On the other hand, if you focus on your faults and weaknesses, distorting failure and imperfections, you have a negative self-image.[6] A negative self-image causes you to doubt your capabilities and ideas.[7] Fortunately, since you are still breathing, your self-image is still developing.

Whether you currently have a positive or negative self-image, you continually take in information and evaluate yourself based on your physical appearance, performance and relationships.[8] These assessments are impactful because they not only affect how you feel about yourself but also how you interact with the world around you.[9]

When I was in high school, I viewed myself as an average student at best. Neither teachers nor my parents took any interest in my schooling or encouraged me to do better. So, I had no idea I could do better than a C average, and I was certainly not motivated in any way to try to do so.

Then one day as I sat in my senior English class, another student shared with me a comment the teacher made to her about my writing. The teacher had assigned us a book report. I read *The Diary of Anne Frank* and received an A on the report, but the teacher never said anything to me about it. Instead, he mentioned to this other student how impressed he was with my writing and the depth of my assessment of the book. I sat stunned when this student shared the teacher's comments with me. Because of that experience, I began thinking I could write and possibly go to college.

It wasn't until some years later, after I married Mike and had three children, that I enrolled in college. Composition was one of my first classes. The professor gave me great feedback about my writing. I began gaining confidence and thinking, "Maybe I do have brains and something to say!" This was another experience that improved my self-image.

But I had plenty of experiences that also caused doubt. I received a sewing machine for my fourteenth birthday and learned how to sew in a Home Economics class. During my senior year of high school, I selected a beautiful, but rather difficult pattern and some lovely fabric for a blouse. I worked hard to make the blouse. The cuffs pointed toward the elbows. I was so proud that both the cuffs and collar were perfectly pointed as they should have been. I proudly showed the blouse to a family member, expecting to be praised for how beautiful it was. Instead, because the fabric pattern was one-sided and the white underside of the fabric could be seen when the collar wasn't buttoned, the family member criticized the blouse and my sewing. That experience caused my self-image to plummet again. I doubted that I could ever sew properly. As a result, I ran to my room, threw the blouse in my closet and didn't sew again until many years later when I began making my children's Halloween costumes.

We all form an image of ourselves that changes over time along with our appearance, abilities and relationships. Fortunately, our self-image doesn't have to go up and down like a roller coaster based on what other people say or do, or how we feel we stack up against someone else's beauty, talents or relationships. These types of assessments are based on ever changing standards, usually based on unwise comparisons, and lead not only to instability in how we view ourselves but also instability in how we conduct our lives. Instead, we need to find that one stable standard--the one that never changes--in order to develop an accurate self-image.

God is the Never-Changing Standard

As I explained to Dad, God is the same yesterday, today, and forever.[10] When we view ourselves through His standard, we can maintain a consistent self-image through our lives. And it will be a right self-image, not a positive or negative one, and it will enable us to have confidence as we interact with the world. We will recognize and focus on the strengths we have in Christ while being realistic about our weaknesses.

When the people of Israel became prideful and self-centered, likely comparing themselves to other people, God spoke through the prophet Jeremiah, reminding them their wisdom, might and riches were not worthy of glory.[11] Instead, God reminded them they should only glory in knowing and understanding Him, who exercises lovingkindness, judgment and righteousness on the earth, because these are what delights the Lord.[12] This is a constant standard to assess ourselves by. Do you know and understand God's lovingkindness, judgment and righteousness? Then as you grow in these attributes of God, you have reason to glory…in Him!

The apostle Paul teaches us a key to having a right self-image. Despite all he had accomplished for God and His Church, Paul refused to glory in himself, because that would be foolish.[13] Instead, he learned to look positively upon his hardships.[14] He had some ailment he called a "thorn in the flesh, the messenger of Satan to buffet me, lest I should be exalted above measure."[15] Three times Paul asked the Lord to remove the thorn from him.[16] And Jesus declined to do so, explaining, "My grace is sufficient for thee: for my strength is made perfect in weakness."[17] Through this Paul learned, and teaches us, not to disdain weaknesses but to glory in them, because through them Christ makes us strong and is glorified.[18]

Another key to having a right self-image is to forget the past and reach for the future. Once we are in relationship with Christ, having salvation by God's grace through faith, we need no longer look at our sinful, hurtful past. Instead, we focus on the hope of eternal life with Jesus that is ahead of us and pursue a deeper relationship with Him.[19] In doing so, we grow in our knowledge of Him, progressively becoming more deeply and intimately acquainted with Him.[20] The apostle Paul describes our identity as Christians.

> For we [Christians] are the true circumcision, who worship God in spirit *and* by the Spirit of God and exult *and* glory *and* pride ourselves in Jesus Christ, and put no confidence *or* dependence [on what we are] in the flesh *and* on outward privileges *and* physical advantages *and* external appearances.[21]

It took me some time to realize who I am in Christ, especially as I began teaching and ministering to adults. Teaching children's Sunday School classes was pretty easy, and I seldom thought myself unworthy or incapable of doing so. Most churches provide curriculum to the teachers of the children's Sunday School classes. It was simple to teach the curriculum. And children tend to shower love on their Sunday School teachers, so I had no reason to doubt myself.

Teaching teenagers was a little more difficult because they don't accept the teachers quite as openly, and they often do not accept the teachings of the Bible. So, when I was asked to teach the teenagers, I found myself looking back on my own teenage years and doubting myself. But the church still provided curriculum to teach, so I hid behind the curriculum and taught the teenagers. To be honest, I loved the teenagers and still do. But at that time, I doubted myself and what I had to offer.

Then the time came when I was asked to teach adults and occasionally minister in the mid-week and Sunday services. That was when the full force of my past began taunting me. There was no curriculum to hide behind. I had to seek God, study His Word and develop every lesson and message I delivered. I was putting myself out for all to see.

Although the people in the classes and the services were always very loving, supportive and accepting of me as a teacher and minister, I had a hard time with doubt and self-criticism. I questioned what I had to offer because I was not raised in a solid Christian home. I was not taught the Bible. I didn't have a Bible School or seminary education. *What did I have to offer?*

During that time, I assessed how well I had spoken by the reaction of those I ministered to. If I received positive comments from people after I spoke, I felt like I did a good job. But if no one responded to me afterwards, the self-doubt crept back in and I was sure I blew it. I also compared the reactions of the people to how they responded to other ministers. There I was, comparing again, which we have already learned does not please God and does not lead to a right self-image.

Then I learned something that changed how I assessed myself and the effectiveness of how I ministered. I had traveled to a conference with my mentor. She gave the message at the conference and opened the altar for prayer. I watched the people at the altar and asked God to lead me to a person who needed someone to pray for and with her. A woman was kneeling on the floor and pouring her heart out to God. I stepped behind her, kneeled and began fervently praying for her. But I noticed she immediately froze. She was no longer seeking God. She was merely kneeling there with her face to the floor. No reaction at all. *Oh, my! What have I done? I've quenched the Spirit!*

The next morning at breakfast I shared the experience with my mentor. She explained to me that we are to never evaluate our impact by other people's reactions. Instead, if we sought God's direction and acted accordingly, then we accomplished His will, which is the goal.

I had no confidence in my own flesh, but I wasn't supposed to! Instead, by no longer looking at my past and lack of credentials, I grew confident in Christ's working through me. I continued seeking Him more and more, to know Him more intimately. As I sought Him, He gave me the words to share with others through individual conversations and through public speaking. Before every speaking engagement I pray, "Lord, I will open my mouth. I ask you to fill it with the words you would have me say."[22] Then after I minister His Word, I need not assess how the people respond. I have complete confidence that His will was accomplished and He was glorified. I retain a right self-image by forgetting the past and focusing on the future with Christ.

It is always helpful to remember that God does not see us as man sees us, so we need not evaluate ourselves through the eyes of other people. When the prophet Samuel was looking for the person God wanted to anoint as the king of Israel after King Saul, God instructed him not to look on the man's countenance or height, "for *the Lord seeth* not as man seeth; for man looketh on the outward appearance, but the Lord looketh on the heart."[23] Our right self-image is not dependent on our outward appearance. Instead, it is what is in our heart. And as we look into a mirror, we behold the glory of the Lord and are changed into that same image by the Spirit of the Lord.[24]

Contemplate Your Self-Image and Adjust It, If Necessary, To Have a Right Self-Image

As you start this time of contemplation, I encourage you to search the Internet for the song recorded by Mark Schultz titled "Father's Eyes."[25] Find the lyrics also and read through them as you listen to the song. The lyrics illustrate how self-image is a problem for both boys and girls, men and women. The first verse is about a seventeen-year-old girl who thinks the mirror is her enemy. And the second verse is about a man ready to give up because he feels shame for not accomplishing things he thought he would and becoming the man he wanted to be. But the chorus answers both of these concerns. In their Father's eyes, they are loved with abandon, safe and accepted. Their Father is running to them with arms open wide and there is nothing either of them can do to change His mind! The same is true for you.

- What do you see in the mirror? Are you happy with it, or do you spend much time and money trying to improve it?

___

___

___

___

___

- Do you have a positive self-image, a negative self-image or a right self-image?

___

___

___

___

___

- What standards are you using to evaluate yourself? Are those standards ever-changing, such as comparisons with the appearance, performance and relationships of other people, or are they constant because they are based on who you are in Christ?

- If you find you do not have a right self-image, consider the scriptures shared in this chapter and begin praying them for yourself and accepting who you are in Christ.

- Spend some time asking God to show you where you view yourself with an incorrect self-image and to show you clearly who you are in Him.

Write the above responses down for further prayerful contemplation. Let God show you how He has fathered you as you read the next chapter about being part of a family.

11

Acceptance:

We Do Not Need to Struggle to Be Part of the Family

Hey Dad, it's me!

Do you remember when I was visiting you and you pulled out a bound book that represented the family tree? The book listed the family relationships of your family for many generations; I don't remember how many. But I do remember holding my breath as you showed me the book. I was afraid to breathe. And I was afraid to ask the obvious question: Am I included in this book?

But I did breathe, and I did ask the question. Since I was adopted by my first stepfather when I was about five, I assumed I would not be included in the book. I was confident no one else, including my adoptive father, would include me in their family tree. Because I did not have a continuing father relationship with anyone else, I needed to find my name in your book. I needed to know I was part of a family.

Once I asked the question, you very easily turned to the page that contained my birth name. I was not only thrilled that my name was written in your book, but I was also more thrilled that you found my name so easily in this three-hundred-plus page book! For the first time I felt like I was part of your family, not just because you are my biological father but also because you wanted me listed as a part of your family regardless of the adoption. Thank you, Dad!

Have you ever heard Randy say that he and I do not have a family tree, but we have a family bush? I always laughed at him when he said it, but it is so true. Just counting the siblings we are related to by blood or adoption, we each have nine siblings. If we add the stepsiblings that came in and out of our lives, we would add another four. It really is more of a bush than a tree. And yet I have never felt I was part of any family except the two siblings I was raised with, which included Randy and our younger sister from our adoptive father.

Dad, I suspect you were aware of my discomfort. However, we never discussed it. Unmistakably, I was treated like a guest when I visited your home from my first visit shortly after I graduated from high school to my last visit when all of your children were adults and had children of their own.

When I was sixteen and you came through my hometown and invited me to meet you at Denny's, I could understand why you might not want to introduce me to your three children. But I don't think I ever understood why you didn't introduce me to your wife, even after she saw me waiting for you outside the restaurant and took me to you. So, from the very start of our relationship I was kept separate from your current family.

Then you invited me to visit you after I graduated from high school. Your children from your second wife were still in school; I suspect they ranged from a sophomore in high school to about fifth grade. They acted as kids do, but we didn't have very much interaction. I really struggled to make a place for myself in your family.

The fact that I was never accepted as part of your family is not something you need to feel guilty about. Even James Dobson acknowledges the difficulty of achieving a successful family, that families are never perfect and are often problematic.[1] There were too many people involved and so few family memories made with me to expect your family to welcome me as more than a guest, or someone to pity as I mentioned in a previous letter. But feeling guilty isn't necessary.

When God fathered me, He welcomed me into His huge family. In His healthy, loving family I have brothers, sisters and elders who guide me like grandparents, parents, aunts and uncles in a healthy, natural family would do. We laugh together. We cry together. We grow together. And we sometimes have to say goodbye to each other when our lives take us down different roads. But most of all, we love and support each other even though we may sometimes have "sibling rivalries" just like any natural family.

Dad, you don't need to feel guilty. God welcomed me into a huge, loving family. I didn't have to struggle to make a place for myself. In His family, I found all of the love, acceptance and guidance I need.

From me, the one who always wanted to be "your little girl!"

The Makings of a Family

Family. What is it?

According to the U.S. Census Bureau, "A family is a group of two people or more (one of whom is the householder) related by birth, marriage, or adoption and residing together."[2] Clearly, based on this definition, I should not have been accepted into Dad's second family because I did not reside with them. Yet, I was related to Dad and his children by birth.

There are many other definitions of "family" under U.S. law. Definitions vary based on the context for which the term is used, such as "for the purpose of determining welfare rights, housing benefits, insurance benefits, healthcare coverage, etc."[3] But most people do not define families according to these objective definitions and, instead, develop their own subjective definition based on relationships.[4]

In subjective definitions of family, biology or legal status is not the ultimate determination of who is included in one's family. Instead, when asked who their family members are, people will likely include those with whom they have quality communication, are emotionally close to, do things for each other and are available as potential helpers in times of need.[5] The one basic similarity among families is a close bond of love and concern for one another.[6]

As an example, a stepmother, especially a residential stepmother, may include her stepchildren in her definition of family because she cares for them, provides for them and sets rules for them when they are in her home. Yet, often the stepchildren do not include their stepmother as a member of their family because they do not have a close relationship with her. They may eat the food and wear the clothes she provides and comply with the rules of her household, but those things do not establish the close, emotional relationship they consider necessary to be part of the family. They likely go to their father for close communication, emotional support and other help when needed.

In my situation, I did not officially meet Dad's second wife (not actually my stepmother because I was not legally Dad's daughter) until I was eighteen. We never shared more than surface level communication, we were never emotionally close and neither of us would think of going to the other in times of need. If asked who our family members are, neither one of us would identify the other. However, depending on the context of the question, if I were asked who my siblings are, I would include Dad's children in his second family while explaining that they are half-siblings even though I am not legally related to them. I suspect, but am not certain, Dad's sons would also identify me in the same manner.

Dana Costache, a family and divorce mediator, asserts that togetherness, both spatial and temporal, is the key to what makes a family.[7] She explains indestructible bonds of family are created when the children are together with their parents throughout most of the first two decades of their lives and the togetherness molds them into who they are as individuals.[8] That is why adult children generally do not lose the "family" connection after they embark on their own independent adult lives. As I write this in 2021, many families with adult children are estranged due to social and political differences and accusations of emotionally abusive upbringings. Yet, if asked who their family members are, likely most of these adult children would still include their estranged parents as family members, and vice versa. That is how strong the family bonds are when established by togetherness during the growing-up years, even if adult children feel that separation is the only way to handle the pain of their past.

It is difficult for a child, even an adult child, to become part of the family when she and the new family have no shared family histories and memories, which are created through togetherness. The struggle is further exacerbated if they have "very different belief systems which may include a different ethnic or educational background, or religion."[9] Yet, with time to develop their own traditions and memories, most stepfamilies can develop emotionally rich and lasting relationships.[10] Unfortunately, as in my situation, when the absent parent and his second family do not reside near his first family, there is no togetherness and little, if any, time to develop such traditions, memories and relationships, leaving a lasting void in the child's life along with the other social challenges discussed in a previous chapter.

Accepted into the Family of God

Have you ever celebrated with a family when they have adopted a child? Oh, what joy abounds! Not just for the parents, but for the child, the judge, the attorney and all who are privileged to be in the courtroom gallery. It is beautiful and joyous when children become part of loving families who have sought them for some time.

I have dear friends who received a child into foster care when he was released from the hospital at birth. He was three when they adopted him. But in those three years my friends loved this child like their own and fought hard to keep him after the courts reunited him with his birth parents. It didn't take long before the reunification failed, and the child was hospitalized due to injuries he sustained while in his biological family's care. Thankfully, the child services agency called my friends and asked if they would take him back. Of course they would. And they drove out of state to join him and care for him at the hospital until he was released into their care.

What a day of celebration it was when we all joined at the courthouse and the judge declared the boy to be their son. The courtroom erupted in applause and happy tears because we all knew the pain and suffering the child had endured when he remained part of his biological family. That pain and suffering was over! He was and is their son, loved, cared for and cherished.

Earthly adoption does not even compare to the joy when a person is adopted into God's family. When we enter into the family of God through faith in Jesus Christ, our Lord and Savior, a "great cloud of witnesses"[11] explodes in rejoicing.

At that time, we receive a spirit of adoption as the Holy Spirit bears witness that we are children of God, and we joyfully cry, "Abba, Father."[12] Like my adopted friend, the pain and suffering caused by being in bondage to the world (our biological family) is over. We are now part of the household of God.[13] We are the children of our heavenly Father, loved, cared for and cherished.

The Function of the Family of God

I realize not all single-parent households are dysfunctional. Nevertheless, many of us who were raised with physically or emotionally absent fathers long to be part of a healthy, functional family. And that is what God offers us when we join His family. He sets us in a church family.[14]

God gives us Christian brothers and sisters to walk through life with us. And like a good Father, He teaches us to be good to one another.[15] And He teaches us to rejoice with each other when one of us is honored.[16] When one of our brothers or sisters suffer, we all suffer together.[17] This is what a healthy, functional family looks like, and we are part of one.

Below is how Brooke Krebill describes her healthy, functional childhood home in her book, *Uncaged: Break Free by Changing Your Inner Story*.

> I don't have a horrible sob story of childhood; I'm one of four kids. We did the regular sibling fights and two minutes later we would be best friends. With two boys and two girls, and with the oldest and the youngest only six years apart, we knew how to fight and how to get along from birth. [. . .] Although my siblings were my first friends, we easily got on each other's nerves as well.
>
> My parents were loving. I have memories of laughing and fighting. I have memories of family dinners. My upbringing was a good one. [. . .] I've been really blessed.[18]

The family God sets us in is very similar to how Ms. Krebill describes her family. We love each other. Many of us share dinners together. And we sometimes encounter sibling rivalry with our Christian brothers and sisters. As an example, the apostle Paul and Barnabas were Christian brothers who traveled together evangelizing. During their first missionary journey, they took with them John Mark, Barnabas's cousin. But John Mark did not complete his commitment to the journey and returned to Jerusalem early.[19] Later, as Paul and Barnabas planned their second missionary journey, Barnabas insisted on taking John Mark with them.[20] Paul disagreed, and the two brothers struggled so sharply they separated company.[21] This is sibling rivalry at a high level!

As a good Father, God teaches us how to handle contentions among our Christian brothers and sisters in a loving, healthy manner. We are to be merciful, kind, humble, meek, patient, forgiving.[22] The Bible indicates that subsequent to Paul's and Barnabas's separation, Paul and John Mark were eventually reunited.[23] The Bible isn't as clear about the relationship between Paul and Barnabas. However, sometime after they had parted ways, Paul seems to mention Barnabas as one of his equals.[24] Therefore, it is reasonable to assume Paul, Barnabas and Mark all employed this manner for resolving disagreements among the brothers.

God even gives us elders to guide us like grandparents, parents, aunts and uncles would in a healthy, natural family. He teaches us to respect our elders, not to rebuke them but rather to encourage them as we would our fathers and mothers.[25] And the elders are to teach the younger generations how to live and conduct themselves.[26] In this family of God, our Father provides us everything we need to live in love, functioning like the healthy family we have longed for, gathering together and encouraging one another.[27]

We are accepted into the family of God. We need not struggle to be part of it. Our Father loves us, provides all we need and teaches us how to function as a loving, healthy family.

Contemplate Your Place in Your Natural Family and in the Family of God

Some of the questions below assume you are a Christian and have been adopted into the family of God. If you have not, I invite you to spend some time in prayer, acknowledging to God your sins and need for a savior. Then seek a pastor and church who can guide you into a relationship with Jesus Christ and adoption into the family of God.

- How do you define your family? Who is included in it?

- Have you struggled to be part of a family? What happened to help you be part, or what keeps you from being part of the family?

- What is your idea of a healthy, functional family?

- How has the family of God been that healthy, functional family for you? Who are your close brothers, sisters, elders who celebrate with you, encourage you and have helped show you the way through this Christian life?

- Spend some time thanking God for being adopted into His family and for His love, acceptance and for cherishing you as His child.

Write the above responses down for further prayerful contemplation. Let God show you how He has fathered you as you read the next chapter about receiving His name.

12

Identity:

He Gives You a Name

Hey Dad, it's me!

In my last letter I shared how important it was to me that my name appeared in your book containing the family tree. I was so happy to see it there, even though it was a name that no longer represented my identity. That caused me to start thinking about how important a name is and how long we retain the names we are given.

When I was born, you gave me your last name. It identified me as your daughter. And I kept that name until I was adopted by my adoptive father. Your name was taken away from me when you signed the adoption papers, and I was no longer legally your daughter.

My name was changed, my birth certificate was changed and my identity was changed. I was now someone else's daughter. I find it amazing that even though I was about five when this happened, I don't remember any of these events. I don't remember ever having your name. I don't remember being told my name was changing. I don't remember sitting in a court room with a judge announcing the adoption. There must not have been any fanfare around it like other adoptions I've witnessed.

When I was eighteen, my name changed again. After saying a few vows, I became someone's wife. I kept that name for only a few short years. Then I became someone else's wife. And I am thrilled to say that I have been identified as his wife for more than forty years, and I don't expect my name and identity to ever change again.

But, Dad, I carry another identity that will last even longer than being Mike's wife. This name and identity do not appear on any legal documents, though it identifies me as a child of God. And I will be a child of God for all eternity. That name is Jesus.

When I was baptized in accordance with Matthew 28:19 and Acts 2:38, I took on Jesus's name when His name was spoken over me. My immersion in the water symbolized the death of my old life and burial with Jesus Christ. And when I came out of the water, I was resurrected into a new life in Christ and born into the family of God. I am and will always be a child of God. I now carry the name of Jesus as part of my identity.

Dad, you need not feel guilty for having signed the adoption papers and taking your last name away from me. Names on earth are so fleeting. So many people are born with one name and are given or choose to take on other names later. But God, the one who has fathered me so beautifully, has given me His name for all eternity.

From me, the one who always wanted to be "your little girl!"

Julie

Julie McGhghy

The Only Permanent Name

Dr. Myles Munroe wrote *The Fatherhood Principle: God's Design and Destiny for Every Man* to help men understand how God designed them. In the book he explains a simple principle of fatherhood: "You provide identity."[1] Dad provided me that identity when I was born with his name. But I only carried that name for about five years. Then my name changed by adoption, and I became someone else's daughter.

Traditionally, in the United States when a woman gets married, she takes on her husband's last name, replacing the last name given to her at birth. Under that tradition the men generally retain their last name. But that tradition has gradually changed over the years. Now a man may take on his wife's name. Or both husband and wife may hyphenate their two names.

Now people can change their names at will by simply filing a name change document with the appropriate state agency accompanied by supporting documentation, such as an adoption certificate, a marriage license or a divorce decree. People who want to change their names for any other reason may have to petition a court. Why? Because their name is a significant part of their identity.

As I explained to Dad, I was first identified as Dad's daughter, then my adoptive father's daughter, then someone's wife. Sharing my husband's last name for over forty years is very precious to me and exceeds anything I ever dreamed possible based on the prevalence of divorce for generations in my family. But the name I cherish most and am thankful will remain with me throughout all eternity is the name of Jesus. I received His name when I was baptized.

The name of Jesus will never change. He declared Himself to be the "Alpha and Omega, the beginning and the end, the first and the last."[2] He is the same yesterday, today and forever.[3] All who are baptized into Jesus's name will carry that name into all eternity and be identified as a child of God.

The Importance of a Name

Some years ago, I was a Privacy Officer for a property and casualty insurance company. At that time, under state laws that pertain to a person's privacy and data security, in order to be considered a breach of security the person's name must be accessed by an unauthorized person along with some other piece of information about the person, such as a social security number, credit card number and PIN, or driver's license number. The reason the name is necessary to qualify as a breach of data security is because identity theft cannot be perpetrated without the person's name. A name identifies a person. It is an important part of each person's identity.

You may remember the lyrics from the popular country music song "Last Name" that was written and performed by Carrie Underwood in 2008.[4] The song is about a woman who had too much to drink, met a man in a bar and eloped with him to Las Vegas. She awoke the next morning and discovered she did not even know her last name, and she recognized that her momma would be very ashamed. Alan Jackson sang about a similar theme in "I Don't Even Know Your Name."[5] But country music does not only include songs about the shame that can be brought on by the mistreatment or neglect of a name, a name that forms part of a person's identity. It also includes songs about honoring a person's name, such as Dierks Bentley's "My Last Name."

> "The narrator describes the origins and the experiences of his last name, such as when he beat up a bully who made fun of his name and when his grandpa 'took it off to Europe to fight the Germans in the war.' In the final verse, the narrator then says that he wants to marry his lover — to give her his last name because he does not have much."[6]

These three songs emphasize the importance of knowing and respecting one's name. This is important because one's name is a large part of one's identity. The same is true about the name into which we are baptized. We must respect the name like Dierks Bentley and be careful not to mistreat, neglect and disrespect the name like Carrie Underwood and Alan Jackson.

From beginning to end in the Old Testament, God gradually revealed Himself to His people. When Moses asked God what he should tell the children of Israel when they asked for the name of the God of their fathers, God told Moses to say, "I AM THAT I AM."[7] At that time, it was enough for God's children to know He existed. But as His relationship with His children developed, God revealed more and more about His name and His character. He had previously shown Himself to Abraham as Jehovah-Jireh, "the Lord will provide."[8] He continued to show Himself to Moses as Jehovah-Rapha, "the Lord our healer,"[9] Jehovah-Nissi, "the Lord our banner,"[10] and Jehovah-Maccaddeshem, "the Lord thy sanctifier."[11]

God didn't stop revealing Himself and His name when Moses died. He showed Himself to Gideon as Jehovah-Shalom, "the Lord is peace,"[12] and to King David as Jehovah-Rohi, "the Lord my shepherd."[13] He also continued revealing Himself and His name to the prophets. To Isaiah, He revealed Himself as Jehovah-Sabboath, "the Lord of Hosts."[14] To Jeremiah, He revealed Himself as Jehovah-Tsidkenu, "the Lord our righteousness"[15] and Jehovah-Gmolah, "the God of recompense."[16] And to Ezekiel, God revealed Himself as Jehovah-Shammah, "the Lord who is present."[17]

Clearly, it was important to God that we know His character and His name. He progressively revealed Himself throughout the Old Testament according to the relationship He fostered with His people. But He didn't stop there! God revealed His name, finally and completely, when He came to earth, robed in flesh and was called Jesus, "the Lord will save."[18]

It is the name of Jesus that is above every name.[19] At the name of Jesus every knee shall bow and every tongue confess that He is Lord.[20] There is salvation in no other, "for there is none other name under heaven given among men, whereby we must be saved."[21]

The name was so important that Jesus commissioned His disciples to baptize people from all nations in His name, which is the "name of the Father, and of the Son, and of the Holy Ghost."[22] On the day of Pentecost, when the crowd asked what they should do, Peter instructed them, in part, to "be baptized [. . .] in the name of Jesus Christ for the remission of sins."[23] Peter's instructions were consistent with Jesus's direction as recorded in Matthew 28:19 and in Luke 24:46-47.[24] Peter preached repentance and remission of sins in Jesus's name. Every baptism for the remission of sins in the book of Acts was done in the name of Jesus, the Lord.[25] And when we are baptized, we take on the name of Jesus and a new identity!

It is important to God that we know His name as He revealed it from the beginning of history, culminating in the name used when He robed Himself in flesh and walked on this earth--the name of Jesus.[26] What a privilege to be baptized in the name of Jesus in order to show due respect for the name and to identify with Him by putting on Christ through baptism.[27] Being baptized in Jesus's name shows proper respect and honor to God as Dierks Bentley showed in his song for the family name he carried on earth.

Contemplate the Names You've Had and the Importance of Having Jesus's Name

I hope you not only understand the importance of your name and how it impacts your identity but also appreciate that importance.

- What last names have you had during your life and how did those names change your identity?

- What does it mean to you that once you took on the name of Jesus, you will be able to keep that name throughout all eternity?

- Spend some time thanking God for identifying you as part of His family when you were baptized.

Write the above responses down for further prayerful contemplation. If you have not taken on the name of Jesus by being baptized, pray about taking that step. Let God show you your true identity as you read the next chapter about God's transforming love.

13

God's Transforming Love:

Turning Regrets into Thanksgiving

Hey Dad, it's me!

Well, I think the time has come for me to acknowledge my regrets. When I started writing to you, I told you I was doing so with the intention of changing things. My desire was to share my heart, and maybe we could get to know each other better. But I must now admit that getting to know you better isn't possible.

Dad, when you died it shook me to my core. When your daughter-in-law called me to tell me you'd had a heart attack and passed away, I couldn't breathe. That isn't an unusual reaction when someone loses a person who is really close to them. But we weren't that close. Why was I so shaken? Your passing would not change anything in my daily life.

After much crying, praying and contemplating, I realized your death was the end of my hope to be "your little girl." I wasn't just grieving you; I was also grieving that hope. I would never be "your little girl."

It was at your funeral that I learned you felt guilty. As I said in a previous letter, I was so shocked. I had never considered that you would feel guilty. I never experienced any bitterness about your not being an active part of my life for so many years.

So, what do I regret? That I didn't know you enough to know you felt guilty. I regret that I didn't try harder to get to know you better while you were alive. I regret that we didn't develop a close father-daughter relationship. And I regret that I didn't share with you all of the things I have now shared in these letters.

But, Dad, I don't want to end this with regrets. I can do nothing about those things now. More important than my regrets are the reasons I am thankful.

What am I thankful for? I am thankful that I am your daughter regardless of what any legal document states. I am thankful I have inherited from you certain physical and nonphysical characteristics, regardless of my big feet. I am thankful I was able to meet your second family and get to know some of them. And I am thankful I've had this opportunity to write about the things I would have told you had I known you felt guilty. I am thankful for every moment we spent together and every word we said to each other. And I am thankful for the last email exchange we had, only a few months before you passed so suddenly. I cherish that email. It is the only record I have of each of us telling the other "I love you." I am so thankful I was able to say that before you passed.

But most of all, Dad, I am thankful that I was not and am not fatherless! I am fathered by the best Father of all. He provides everything a good father would provide. He does everything a good father would do. And He exceeds what any earthly father can provide or do.

From me, the one who will never be "your little girl," but will always be a child of God.

Julie McGhghy

The Effects of Lingering Emotions

For those of us who have lived with a physically or emotionally absent father, we have all kinds of emotions likely still stirring within us. For me, when thinking about Dad, I feel regret. Regret occurs when people believe they could have had a better outcome if they had acted differently in the past.[1] Often it causes the people experiencing regret to blame themselves even if the alternate behavior was improbable or impossible.[2] And because people feeling regret often also feel shame, sadness or remorse, regret can impede their happiness.[3] But we don't have to live under the shadow of regret.

Jesus does not want us to live with regret. Just as He did for the apostle Peter, He will help restore us to the joyful life He wants us to have if we turn to Him. You may remember when Jesus was arrested in the Garden of Gethsemane, Peter followed from a distance.[4] And because Peter was afraid, he denied Christ three times, just as Jesus had said he would.[5] Upon remembering Jesus's words to him, Peter immediately regretted what he had done, and he wept bitterly.[6]

After Jesus's resurrection, He appeared to His disciples on the shore of the sea of Tiberias.[7] After they shared a meal together, Jesus turned to Peter and asked him three times, "Do you love me?"[8] Each time after Peter responded, Jesus let him know He still had a purpose for him. Jesus instructed Peter to feed His sheep.[9]

If you find you regret things you said or did, or didn't say or do, because of your absent father, Jesus wants to restore your joy and give you a purpose, just as He did for Peter. Just turn to Him and ask Him to restore your joy.[10]

You may also feel anger toward the absent father or others who perpetrated unthinkable things against you in part because your father wasn't there to protect you. If so, remember Joseph's attitude when he was reunited with his brothers.

Joseph's brothers had sold him into slavery when he was young.[11] Many years later, after Joseph was falsely accused of sexual misconduct against Potiphar's wife and was thrown into prison,[12] and then elevated again to be a ruler under Pharaoh,[13] Joseph's brothers visited Egypt to buy food because of a famine.[14] Clearly, seeing his brothers again was very emotional for Joseph, and he struggled to control his feelings.[15]

Joseph had all the power of Egypt to treat his brothers any way he chose to. He could have sought vengeance by beating, torturing or killing them. But, instead, Joseph showed them grace. After their father died and Joseph's brothers feared what Joseph might do to them, Joseph responded, "Fear not: for *am* I in the place of God? But as for you, ye thought evil against me: *but* God meant it unto good, to bring to pass, as *it is* this day, to save much people alive. Now therefore fear ye not: I will nourish you, and your little ones. And he comforted them, and spake kindly unto them."[16]

There are many other emotions you may feel: bitterness, fear and so many more. Extending grace towards those who harmed you like Joseph extended to his brothers releases you to enjoy a rich life of peace. In and of ourselves such a gracious attitude is impossible to attain. And yet God will help you. Claiming the promise "that all things work together for good to them that love God, to them who are the called according to *his* purpose"[17] will help you move forward in grace.

It is also helpful to remember the apostle Paul taught the church in Ephesus to put all bitterness and wrath and anger away from them.[18] But when you have lived life with an absent father, that isn't always easy to do. It can't be done without God's help.

God wants to relieve you from all of these destructive emotions. The key is turning to Him. Ask Him to search you, know your heart and thoughts and lead you away from the feelings that are contrary to what He would want for you and lead you in the paths of righteousness.[19]

After you have sought God's help with these lingering emotions resulting from your past, then the key to peace is prayer and thanksgiving: "Be careful for nothing; but in every thing by prayer and supplication with thanksgiving let your requests be made known unto God. And the peace of God, which passeth all understanding, shall keep your hearts and minds through Christ Jesus."[20] Then you will be able to say like the apostle Paul, "I count not myself to have apprehended: but *this* one thing *I do*, forgetting those things which are behind, and reaching forth unto those things which are before."[21]

Contemplate Your Continuing Emotions and Let Jesus Restore Your Joy

How freeing it is to let go of the past and the resulting lingering emotions. Remember the old hymn.

> Turn your eyes upon Jesus,
> Look full in His wonderful face,
> And the things of earth will grow strangely dim,
> In the light of His glory and grace.[22]

- Spend some time focusing on these lyrics.
- Identify the lingering emotions you still carry.

_____

_____

_____

_____

- Ask God to search you, know your heart and thoughts and lead you away from any feelings that are contrary to what He would want for you.

- List those things you are thankful for, even as relates to your absent father.

Write the above responses down for further prayerful contemplation. Let God restore your joy.

"Now the God of hope fill you with all joy and peace in believing, that ye may abound to hope, through the power of the Holy Ghost."[23]

Acknowledgments

As I began prayerfully exploring what it would take to write a book, I heard much about the solitary process and how writers lock themselves in their rooms for hours as they face the task alone. Although it is true, I spent many hours alone at my desk in Costa Rica during the COVID-19 pandemic facing the experiences of my past, aligning them with God's Word, and putting it all on paper, I found the actual process was much more of a team endeavor than an isolated one. And now my heart wishes to thank all of those who contributed to the process and encouraged me along the way. But doing so is an impossible task because there were so many people. So, I will limit my expressions of gratitude to those who actively participated with me.

I had a group of friends who read all or some part of the manuscript and provided valuable critique: Diane Beall, Samantha Campbell, Randa Chance, Reverend Kristen Ellis, Mickey Gardiner, Sharon Mullen and Seidy Wong. Thank you, ladies, for your time, suggestions and encouragement. I would not have made it to the end without it.

Chad Allen is an amazing writing coach and assembles a wonderful group of writers in the BookCamp Community who encourage each other and give feedback throughout the writing process. Many thanks to all of you.

The Self-Publishing School Mastermind Community is beyond compare! Sharing successes, challenges and recommendations among fellow writers is priceless. This book would not have been completed and found its place in the world without all of you. Thank you.

The Calvary Church in Cincinnati, Ohio! Oh, how you have contributed greatly to this book, yet many of you don't even realize it. Before I was a writer, I was a teacher. And you were all so loving and encouraging as I developed my teaching skills. It is because of the years I taught and you listened and encouraged that I was able to learn so much about God and how to pull many biblical concepts together to see an accurate picture of who He is. Thank you to the fabulous leaders of the church, including the larger-than-life Bishop Norman R. Paslay II who passed to his eternal reward on March 24, 2018, who believed in me and gave me opportunity to grow as a teacher and minister. And I greatly appreciate the love, acceptance and encouragement of the congregation.

My children and husband deserve many thanks also. Without them I would not have been able to fill the pages with so many great examples of the lessons God taught me. Thank you for letting me share a small part of your stories with the world.

I would be remiss if I didn't thank the "family bush"! Although the parts you've all played in my life vary in quantity and quality, there is no mistake that your being a part of the "bush" impacted my life and how I view God. Thank you.

Above all, precious Jesus, thank you for loving me, drawing me, guiding me, protecting me, speaking to me, setting this project before me, and sitting with me in the otherwise lonely room as I researched and wrote this book about You. Although the story is couched in my experiences, the book is all about You, Lord! You are the greatest Father anyone could have and a fatherly relationship with you is available to all. Thank you.

Did you find this book helpful? Maybe you even loved the book and think other people would also find it helpful.

If so, don't forget to leave a review!

Every review matters. And it matters a *lot!*

Head over to Amazon or wherever you purchased this book to leave an honest review for me.

I greatly appreciate your time in reading the book and your insights as you post a review.

Julie McGhghy

Notes

1 Reaching Out: Introducing My Heavenly Father

1. Susan Krauss Whitbourne, "The Definitive Guide to Guilt: Five Types of Guilt and How You Can Cope with Each," Psychology Today, accessed May 13, 2021, https://www.psychologytoday.com/us/blog/fulfillment-any-age/201208/the-definitive-guide-guilt.
2. Ibid.
3. "And we know that all things work together for good to them that love God, to them who are the called according to *his* purpose." Rom. 8:28.
4. Ben Cerullo, "Seeing with the Eyes of Faith," Inspiration Ministries, accessed May 13, 2021, https://inspiration.org/christian-articles/eyes-of-faith/.
5. "Behold, what manner of love the Father hath bestowed upon us, that we should be called the sons of God." 1 John 3:1.
6. "For unto us a child is born, unto us a son is given: [. . .] and his name shall be called [. . .] The everlasting Father." Isa. 9:6.
7. 2 Cor. 3:18.
8. Gal. 5:22–23.
9. Jer. 31:3.
10. "See what great love the Father has lavished on us, that we should be called children of God! And that is what we are!" 1 John 3:1 (NIV).
11. "And the Lord God said, Behold, the man is become as one of us, to know good and evil: and now, lest he put forth his hand, and take also of the tree of life, and eat, and live for ever: Therefore the Lord God sent him forth from the garden of Eden, to till the ground from whence he was taken. So he drove out the man: and he placed at the east of the garden of Eden Cherubims, and a flaming sword which turned every way, to keep the way of the tree of life." Gen. 3:22–24; "Wherefore, as by one man sin entered into the world, and death by sin: and so death passed upon all men, for that all have sinned." Rom. 5:12.
12. "But God commendeth his love toward us, in that, while we were yet sinners, Christ died for us." Rom. 5:8; "And He [that same Jesus Himself] is the propitiation (the atoning sacrifice) for our sins, and not for ours alone but also for [the sins of] the whole world."

1 John 2:2 (AMP; brackets in the original).
13. "God setteth the solitary in families." Ps. 68:6.
14. "As we have therefore opportunity, let us do good unto all *men*, especially unto them who are of the household of faith." Gal. 6:10.
15. "Or one member be honoured, all the members rejoice with it." 1 Cor. 12:26.
16. "And whether one member suffer, all the members suffer with it." 1 Cor. 12:26.
17. "A new commandment I give unto you, That ye love one another; as I have loved you, that ye also love one another." John 13:34.
18. "Rebuke not an elder, but entreat *him* as a father, *and* the younger men as brethren; The elder women as mothers; the younger as sisters, with all purity." 1 Tim. 5:1–2.
19. "That the aged men be sober, grave, temperate, sound in faith, in charity, in patience. The aged women likewise, that *they be* in behaviour as becometh holiness, not false accusers, not given to much wine, teachers of good things; That they may teach the young women to be sober, to love their husbands, to love their children, *To be* discreet, chaste, keepers at home, good, obedient to their own husbands, that the word of God be not blasphemed." Titus 2:2–5.
20. "And let us consider one another to provoke unto love and to good works: Not forsaking the assembling of ourselves together [. . .] but exhorting *one another*." Heb. 10:24–25.
21. "Put on therefore, as the elect of God, holy and beloved, bowels of mercies, kindness, humbleness of mind, meekness, longsuffering: Forbearing one another, and forgiving one another, if any man have a quarrel against any: even as Christ forgave you, so also *do* ye." Col. 3:12–13.

2 Inherited Characteristics: We Will Be Like Him

1. Amy Grant, "Father's Eyes," *My Father's Eyes*, Myrrh Records, released 1979.
2. "Fear thou not; for I *am* with thee: be not dismayed; for I *am* thy God: I will strengthen thee; yea, I will help thee; yea, I will uphold thee with the right hand of my righteousness." Isa. 41:10.
3. "I will instruct thee and teach thee in the way which thou shalt go: I will guide thee with mine eye." Ps. 32:8.
4. "The Facts of Life – Season 1, Episode 10," Television of Yore, accessed May 17, 2021, https://www.televisionofyore.com/recaps-of-the-facts-of-life/the-facts-of-life-season-1-episode-10.
5. Ibid.
6. "Mental health refers to your ability to process information. Emotional health, on the other hand, refers to your ability to express feelings which are based upon the information you have processed." Andrea Herron, "The Emotional and Mental Aspects of Well-Being," WebMD Health Services, accessed May 17, 2021, https://www.webmd-

healthservices.com/2017/07/12/the-emotional-and-mental-aspects-of-well-being/.

7   "Be ye followers of me, even as I also *am* of Christ." 1 Cor. 11:1; "He that saith he abideth in him [Jesus] ought himself also so to walk, even as he walked." 1 John 2:6; "For even hereunto were ye called: because Christ also suffered for us, leaving us an example, that ye should follow his steps." 1 Pet. 2:21.

8   Eph. 5:1–2.

9   "For I have given you an example, that ye should do as I have done to you." John 13:15; "A new commandment I give unto you, That ye love one another; as I have loved you, that ye also love one another." John 13:34; "This is my commandment, That ye love one another, as I have loved you." John 15:12.

10 "For unto us a child is born, unto us a son is given: and the government shall be upon his shoulder: and his name shall be called Wonderful, Counsellor, The mighty God, The everlasting Father, The Prince of Peace." Is. 9:6.

11 John 14:9.

12 "Who is the image of the invisible God, the firstborn of every creature." Col. 1:15.

13 "For in him dwelleth all the fulness of the Godhead bodily." Col. 2:9.

14 "For whom he did foreknow, he also did predestinate *to be* conformed to the image of his Son, that he might be the firstborn among many brethren." Rom. 8:29.

15 "He that spared not his own Son, but delivered him up for us all, how shall he not with him also freely give us all things?" Rom. 8:32.

16 "Bless *be* the God and Father of our Lord Jesus Christ, who hath blessed us with all spiritual blessings in heavenly *places* in Christ: According as he hath chosen us in him before the foundation of the world, that we should be holy and without blame before him in love: Having predestinated us unto the adoption of children by Jesus Christ to himself, according to the good pleasure of his will. To the praise of the glory of his grace, wherein he hath made us accepted in the beloved." Eph. 1:3–6.

17 "And he said unto her, What wilt thou? She saith unto him, Grant that these my two sons may sit, the one on thy right hand, and the other on the left, in thy kingdom. [. . .] And whosoever will be chief among you, let him be your servant: Even as the Son of man came not to be ministered unto, but to minister, and to give his life a ransom for many." Matt. 20:21, 27–28.

18 "If I then, *your* Lord and Master, have washed your feet; ye also ought to wash one another's feet. For I have given you an example, that ye should do as I have done to you." John 13:14–15.

19 "A new commandment I give unto you, That ye love one another; as I have loved you, that ye also love one another." John 13:34.

20 "For even hereunto were ye called: because Christ also suffered for us, leaving us an example, that we should follow his steps: Who did no sin, neither was guile found in his

mouth: Who, when he was reviled, reviled not again; when he suffered, he threatened not; but committed *himself* to him that judgeth righteously." 1 Pet. 2:21–23.

21 "He that saith he abideth in him [Christ] ought himself also so to walk, even as he walked." 1 John 2:6.

22 "Hereby perceive we the love *of God*, because he laid down his life for us: and we out to lay down *our* lives for the brethren." 1 John 3:16.

23 1 Cor. 11:1.

24 "And walk in love, as Christ also hath loved us." Eph. 5:2; "Forbearing one another, and forgiving one another, if any man have a quarrel against any: even as Christ forgave you, so also *do* ye." Col. 3:13.

25 "Thou shalt also consider in thine heart, that, as a man chasteneth his son, *so* the Lord thy God chasteneth thee." Deut. 8:5.

26 "All scripture *is* given by inspiration of God, and *is* profitable for doctrine, for reproof, for correction, for instruction in righteousness: That the man of God may be perfect, thoroughly furnished unto all good works." 2 Tim. 3:16–17.

27 Ibid.

28 "Moreover, we have had earthly fathers who disciplined us and we yielded [to them] *and* respected [them for training us]. Shall we not much more cheerfully submit to the Father of spirits and so [truly] live? For [our earthly fathers] disciplined us for only a short period of time *and* chastised us as seemed proper *and* good to them; but He disciplines us for our certain good, that we may become sharers in His own holiness." Heb. 12:9–10 (AMP; brackets in the original).

29 Ibid.

30 "For whom the Lord loveth he correcteth; even as a father the son *in whom* he delighteth." Prov. 3:12.

31 "If any of you lack wisdom, let him ask of God, that giveth to all *men* liberally, and upbraideth not; and it shall be given him." James 1:5.

32 "Thus saith the Lord, The heaven *is* my throne, and the earth *is* my footstool." Isaiah 66:1; "Nor by the earth; for it is his footstool." Matt. 5:35.

33 "And not only *so*, but we glory in tribulations also: knowing that tribulation worketh patience; And patience, experience; and experience, hope: And hope maketh not ashamed; because the love of God is shed abroad in our hearts by the Holy Ghost which is given unto us." Rom. 5:3–5.

34 Ibid.

35 "My brethren, count it all joy when ye fall into divers temptations; Knowing *this*, that the trying of your faith worketh patience. But let patience have *her* perfect work, that ye may be perfect and entire, wanting nothing." James 1:2–4.

36 "But the fruit of the Spirit is love, joy, peace, longsuffering, gentleness, goodness, faith,

meekness, temperance; against such there is no law." Gal. 5:22–23.

37 "Bless *be* the God and Father of our Lord Jesus Christ, who hath blessed us with all spiritual blessings in heavenly *places* in Christ: According as he hath chosen us in him before the foundation of the world, that we should be holy and without blame before him in love: Having predestinated us unto the adoption of children by Jesus Christ to himself, according to the good pleasure of his will. To the praise of the glory of his grace, wherein he hath made us accepted in the beloved." Eph. 1:3–6.

38 "But we all, with open face beholding as in a glass the glory of the Lord, are changed into the same image from glory to glory, *even* as by the Spirit of the Lord." 2 Cor. 3:18.

3 Unconditional Love: He Loves You with an Everlasting Love

1   Meg Meeker, *Strong Fathers, Strong Daughters: 10 Secrets Every Father Should Know*, quoting Oswald Chambers (New York: Ballantine Books, 2007), 59.
2   James Dobson, *Bringing Up Girls: Shaping the Next Generation of Women* (Carol Stream, IL: Tyndale Momentum, 2010).
3   Ibid, 19, quoting John and Stasi Eldredge, *Captivating: Unveiling the Mystery of a Woman's Soul* (Nashville: Thomas Nelson, 2005), 46.
4   "A father of the fatherless [...] *is* God in his holy habitation." Ps. 68:5.
5   "The Lord taketh pleasure in them that fear him, in those that hope in his mercy." Ps. 147:11; "For the Lord taketh pleasure in his people: he will beautify the meek with salvation." Ps. 149:4.
6   "Behold, you are beautiful, my love! Behold, you are beautiful! You have doves' eyes." Song of Sol. 1:15 (AMP); "[He exclaimed] O my love, how beautiful you are! There is no flaw in you!" Song of Sol. 4:7 (AMP; brackets in the original).
7   "The Lord hath appeared of old unto me, *saying*, Yea, I have loved thee with an everlasting love: therefore with lovingkindness have I drawn thee." Jer. 31:3.
8   1 John 3:1 (NIV).
9   "The Lord is not slow in keeping his promise, as some understand slowness. He is patient with you, not wanting anyone to perish, but everyone to come to repentance." 2 Pet. 3:9 (NIV).
10 "Fear not; for thou shalt not be ashamed: neither be thou confounded; for thou shalt not be put to shame: for thou shalt forget the shame of thy youth, and shalt not remember the reproach of thy widowhood any more." Isa. 54:4.
11 "And we know that all things work together for good to them that love God, to them who are the called according to *his* purpose." Rom. 8:28.
12 "For God so loved the world, that he gave his only begotten Son, that whosoever believeth in him should not perish, but have everlasting life." John 3:16.
13 "See what great love the Father has lavished on us, that we should be called children of

God! And that is what we are!" 1 John 3:1 (NIV).
14. "But as many as received him, to them gave he power to become the sons of God, *even* to them that believe on his name." John 1:12.
15. "And if children, then heirs; heirs of God, and joint-heirs with Christ; if so be that we suffer with *him*, that we may be also glorified together." Rom. 8:17.
16. "And the glory which thou gavest me I have given them; that they may be one, even as we are one." John 17:22.
17. "For ye know the grace of our Lord Jesus Christ, that, though he was rich, yet for your sakes he became poor, that ye through his poverty might be rich." 2 Cor. 8:9.
18. "Hath in these last days spoken unto us by *his* Son, whom he hath appointed heir of all things, by whom also he made the worlds." Heb. 1:2.
19. "To an inheritance incorruptible, and undefiled, and that fadeth not away, reserved in heaven for you." 1 Pet. 1:4.
20. "I marvel that ye are so soon removed from him that called you into the grace of Christ unto another gospel." Gal. 1:6.
21. "And this is his commandment, That we should believe on the name of his son Jesus Christ, and love one another, as he gave us commandment. And he that keepeth his commandments dwelleth in him, and he in him. And hereby we know that he abideth in us, by the Spirit which he hath given us." 1 John 3:23–24.
22. "For he knoweth our frame: he remebereth that we are dust." Ps. 103:14.
23. "O Lord, thou hast searched me, and known me. Thou knowest my downsitting and mine uprising, thou understandest my thought afar off. Thou compassest my path and my lying down, and art acquainted *with* all my ways. For *there is* not a word in my tongue, *but*, lo, O Lord, thou knowest it altogether." Ps. 139:1–4.

4 Religion Versus Christianity: How We Live the Difference
1. "Religion vs. Christianity," The Church on the Corner, accessed May 17, 2021, https://churchonthecorner.us/questions-on-faith/religion-vs-christianity/.
2. Mike Mazzalongo, "What Other Religions Teach About Salvation," BibleTalk, accessed May 17, 2021, https://bibletalk.tv/what-other-religions-teach-about-salvation.
3. "What is the meaning of: merging with Brahman after Moksha?" Hinduism Stack Exchange, accessed May 17, 2021, https://hinduism.stackexchange.com/questions/37754/what-is-the-meaning-of-merging-with-brahman-after-moksha.
4. "Hinduism," Wikimedia Foundation, accessed May 17, 2021, https://en.wikipedia.org/wiki/Hinduism.
5. Ibid.
6. Mazzalongo, "What Other Religions Teach."
7. "For by grace are ye saved through faith; and that not of yourselves; *it is* the gift of God.

Not of works, lest any man should boast." Eph. 2:8–9.
8. John 3:16.
9. "And, having made peace through the blood of his cross, by him to reconcile all things unto himself; by him, *I say*, whether *they be* things in earth, or things in heaven. And you, that were sometime alienated and enemies in *your* mind by wicked works, yet now hath he reconciled in the body of his flesh through death, to present you holy and unblameable and unreproveable in his sight: If ye continue in the faith grounded and settled, and *be* not moved away from the hope of the gospel, which ye have heard, *and* which was preached to every creature which is under heaven; whereof I Paul am made a minister." Col. 1:20–23.
10. "And thou shalt love the Lord thy God with all thy heart, and with all thy soul, and with all thy mind, and with all thy strength: this *is* the first commandment." Matt. 22:37 and Mark 12:30; "Thou shalt love the Lord thy God with all thy heart, and with all thy soul, and with all thy strength, and with all thy mind; and thy neighbour as thyself." Luke 10:27.
11. "And thou shalt love the Lord thy God with all thine heart, and with all thy soul, and with all thy might." Deut. 6:5.
12. Deut. 6:3.
13. "By the which will we are sanctified through the offering of the body of Jesus Christ once *for all*." *The MacArthur New Testament Commentary* on Matthew 6 and citing Heb. 10:10, quoted in "Is Fasting a Command?," Grace to You, accessed May 7, 2021, https://www.gty.org/library/bibleqnas-library/QA0151/is-fasting-a-command.
14. "And they mourned, and wept, and fasted until even, for Saul, and for Jonathan his son, and for the people of the Lord, and for the house of Israel; because they were fallen by the sword." 2 Sam. 1:12; "And it came to pass, when I heard these words, that I sat down and wept, and mourned *certain* days, and fasted, and prayed before the God of heaven." Neh. 1:4.
15. "As they ministered to the Lord, and fasted, the Holy Ghost said, Separate me Barnabas and Saul for the work whereunto I have called them. And when they had fasted and prayed, and laid *their* hands on them, they sent *them* away." Acts 13:2–3; "And when they had ordained them elders in every church, and had prayed with fasting, they commended them to the Lord, on whom they believed." Acts 14:23.
16. "Go, gather together all the Jews that are present in Shushan, and fast ye for me, and neither eat nor drink three days, night or day: I also and my maidens will fast likewise; and so will I go in unto the king, which *is* not according to the law: and if I perish, I perish." Est. 4:16.
17. "And he was there with the Lord forty days and forty nights; he did neither eat bread, nor drink water. And he wrote upon the tables the words of the covenant, the ten com-

mandments." Exod. 34:28.

18 "And I set my face unto the Lord God, to seek by prayer and supplications, with fasting, and sackcloth, and ashes: And I prayed unto the Lord my God, and made my confession, and said, O Lord, the great and dreadful God, keeping the covenant and mercy to them that love him, and to them that keep his commandments; We have sinned, and have committed iniquity, and have done wickedly, and have rebelled, even by departing from thy precepts and from thy judgments: [. . .] O Lord, according to all they righteousness, I beseech thee, let thine anger and thy fury be turned away from thy city Jerusalem, thy holy mountain: because for our sins, and for the iniquities of our fathers, Jerusalem and thy people *are become* a reproach to all *that are* about us. Now therefore, O our God, hear the prayer of thy servant, and his supplications, and cause thy face to shine upon thy sanctuary that is desolate, for the Lord's sake. O my God, incline thine ear, and hear; open thine eyes, and behold our desolations, and the city which is called by thy name: for we do not present our supplications before thee for our righteousnesses, but for thy great mercies. O Lord, hear; O Lord, forgive; O Lord, hearken and do; defer not, for thine own sake, O my God: for thy city and thy people are called by thy name." Dan. 9:3–5, 16–19.

19 Grace to You, "Is Fasting a Command?"

20 William B. Coker Sr., *Words of Endearment: The Ten Commandments as a Revelation of God's Love*, (sermontobook.com, 2020), 235.

21 Ibid.

22 "Wherefore have we fasted, *say they*, and thou seest not? *wherefore* have we afflicted our soul, and thou takest no knowledge? Behold, in the day of your fast ye find pleasure, and exact all your labours. Behold, ye fast for strife and debate, and to smite with the fist of wickedness: ye shall not fast as *ye do this* day, to make your voice to be heard on high. Is it such a fast that I have chosen? a day for a man to afflict his soul? *Is it* to bow down his head as a bulrush, and to spread sackcloth and ashes *under him*? wilt thou call this a fast, and an acceptable day to the Lord?" Isa. 58:3–5.

23 Isa. 58:4.

24 "And he spake this parable unto certain which trusted in themselves that they were righteous, and despised others: Two men went up into the temple to pray; the one a Pharisee, and the other a publican. The Pharisee stood and prayed thus with himself, God, I thank thee, that I am not as other men *are*, extortioners, unjust, adulterers, or even as this publican. I fast twice in the week, I give tithes of all that I possess. And the publican, standing afar off, would not lift up so much as *his* eyes unto heaven, but smote upon his breast, saying, God be merciful to me a sinner. I tell you, this man went down to his house justified *rather* than the other: for every one that exalteth himself shall be abased; and he that humbleth himself shall be exalted." Luke 18:9–14.

25 "The Pharisee stood and prayed thus with himself, God, I thank thee, that I am not as other men *are*, extortioners, unjust, adulterers, or even as this publican." Luke 18:11.
26 "I fast twice in the week, I give tithes of all that I possess." Luke 18:12.
27 "And the publican, standing afar off, would not lift up so much as *his* eyes unto heaven, but smote upon his breast, saying, God be merciful to me a sinner." Luke 18:13.
28 "I tell you, this man went down to his house justified *rather* than the other: for every one that exalteth himself shall be abased; and he that humbleth himself shall be exalted." Luke 18:14.
29 "No forsaking the assembling of ourselves together, as the manner of some *is*; but exhorting *one another*: and so much the more, as ye see the day approaching." Heb. 10:25.
30 "Bring ye all the tithes into the storehouse, that there may be meat in mine house, and prove me now herewith, saith the Lord of hosts, if I will not open you the windows of heaven, and pour you out a blessing, that *there shall not be room* enough *to receive it*." Mal. 3:10.
31 "And the second *is* like unto it, Thou shalt love thy neighbour as thyself." Matt. 22:39.
32 "All unrighteousness is sin: and there is a sin not unto death." 1 John 5:17.
33 "For the joy of the Lord is your strength." Neh. 8:10.
34 Jay Payleitner, *52 Things Daughters Need From Their Dads: What Fathers Can Do to Build a Lasting Relationship* (Eugene, OR: Harvest House Publishers, 2013), 91.
35 Meeker, *Strong Fathers, Strong Daughters*, 193.
36 Ibid.
37 "No man can come to me, except the Father which hath sent me draw him: and I will raise him up at the last day." John 6:44.
38 Curt Dodd, "God Draws Us to Himself," Higher Aim Ministries, accessed May 18, 2021, https://higheraim.org/2020/03/16/god-draws-us-to-himself/.
39 "All scripture *is* given by inspiration of God, and *is* profitable for doctrine, for reproof, for correction, for instruction in righteousness: That the man of God may be perfect, thoroughly furnished unto all good works." 2 Tim. 3:16–17.
40 "However, I am telling you nothing but the truth when I say it is profitable (good, expedient, advantageous) for you that I go away. Because if I do not go away, the Comforter (Counselor, Helper, Advocate, Intercessor, Strengthener, Standby) will not come to you [into close fellowship with you]; but if I go away, I will send Him to you [to be in close fellowship with you]. And when He comes, He will convict *and* convince the world *and* bring demonstration to it about sin and about righteousness (uprightness of heart and right standing with God) and about judgment." John 16:7–8 (AMP; brackets in the original).
41 Meeker, *Strong Fathers, Strong Daughters*, 178.
42 Ibid.

43 Ibid.
44 Ibid, citing Christian Smith with Melinda Lundquist Denton, *Soul Searching: The Religious and Spiritual Lives of American Teenagers* (New York: Oxford University Press, 2005), 218–64.
45 Ibid, citing Christian Smith with Melinda Lundquist Denton, *Soul Searching: The Religious and Spiritual Lives of American Teenagers* (New York: Oxford University Press, 2005), 151–152.
46 Ibid, citing Christian Smith with Melinda Lundquist Denton, *Soul Searching: The Religious and Spiritual Lives of American Teenagers* (New York: Oxford University Press, 2005), 153.

5 Authority Figure: He Is the Source of Our Support and Guidance
1 "Whether therefore ye eat, or drink, or whatsoever ye do, do all to the glory of God." 1 Cor. 10:31.
2 Meeker, *Strong Fathers, Strong Daughters*, 38.
3 Meeker, *Strong Fathers, Strong Daughters*, 38–39.
4 Jer. 32:27.
5 1 Chron. 29:11.
6 Job 42:2.
7 "Come unto me, all *ye* that labour and are heavy laden, and I will give you rest." Matt. 11:28.
8 "Humble yourselves therefore under the mighty hand of God, that he may exalt you in due time: Casting all your care upon him; for he careth for you." 1 Pet. 5:6–7.
9 "Be careful for nothing; but in every thing by prayer and supplication with thanksgiving let your requests be made known unto God. And the peace of God, which passeth all understanding, shall keep your hearts and minds through Christ Jesus." Phil. 4:6–7.
10 Jer. 18:1–6.
11 Isa. 64:8.
12 "Trust in the Lord with all thine heart; and lean not unto thine own understanding. In all thy ways acknowledge him, and he shall direct thy paths." Prov. 3:5–7.

6 Boundaries: God's Loving Source of Security
1 Meeker, *Strong Fathers, Strong Daughters*, 208.
2 Ibid.
3 Coker, *Words of Endearment*, 234.
4 Coker, *Words of Endearment*, 11–12, 232–233.
5 Coker, *Words of Endearment*, 24–25, 186.
6 Coker, *Words of Endearment*, 170.

7   Ibid.
8   "Then one of them [Pharisees], *which was* a lawyer, asked *him a question*, tempting him, and saying, Master, which *is* the great commandment in the law? Jesus said unto him, Thou shalt love the Lord thy God with all thy heart, and with all thy soul, and with all thy mind. This is the first and great commandment. And the second *is* like unto it, Thou shalt love thy neighbour as thyself. On these two commandments hang all the law and the prophets." Matt. 22:35–40; see also Mark 12:28–31.
9   Coker, *Words of Endearment*, 170.
10 Matt. 5:3–7:27.

7 Beyond the Boundaries: God's Protection
1   2 Thess. 3:3 (NIV).
2   Cerullo, "Seeing with the Eyes of Faith."
3   "That ye may be the children of your Father which is in heaven: for he maketh his sun to rise on the evil and on the good, and sendeth rain on the just and on the unjust." Matt. 5:45.
4   Coker, *Words of Endearment*, 132.
5   John 10:28–30.
6   Rom. 8:35–39.
7   "Be strong and of a good courage, fear not, nor be afraid of them: for the Lord thy God, he *it is* that doth go with thee; he will not fail thee, nor forsake thee." Deut. 31:6.
8   "Fear thou not; for I *am* with thee: be not dismayed; for I *am* thy God: I will strengthen thee; yea, I will help thee; yea, I will uphold thee with the right hand of my righteousness." Isa. 41:10.
9   "God *is* our refuge and strength, a very present help in time of trouble." Ps. 46:1.
10 "Fear not; for thou shalt not be ashamed: neither be thou confounded; for thou shalt not be put to shame: for thou shalt forget the shame of thy youth, and shalt not remember the reproach of thy widowhood any more." Isa. 54:4.
11 Barbara Hughes, "Where Was God? Spiritual Questions of Sexually Abused Children," Center for Children and Theology, accessed February 16, 2021, https://cctheo.org/occasional-papers/where-was-god-spiritual-questions-sexually-abused-children.
12 Ibid.
13 Ibid.
14 "And we know that all things work together for good to them that love God, to them who are the called according to *his* purpose." Rom. 8:28.
15 "Whereof I Paul am made a minister; Who now rejoice in my sufferings for you, and fill up that which is behind of the afflictions of Christ in my flesh for his body's sake, which is the church." Col. 1:23–24.

16 "That I may know him, and the power of his resurrection, and the fellowship of his sufferings, being made conformable unto his death." Phil. 3:10.
17 "If by any means I might attain unto the resurrection of the dead." Phil. 3:11.
18 "Keep me, O Lord, from the hands of the wicked; preserve me from the violent man; who have purposed to overthrow my goings." Ps. 140:4.
19 "We *are* troubled on every side, yet not distressed; we *are* perplexed, but not in despair; Persecuted, but not forsaken; cast down, but not destroyed." 2 Cor. 4:8–9.
20 "God *is* our refuge and strength, a very present help in trouble." Ps. 46:1.
21 "Therefore will not we fear, though the earth be removed, and though the mountains be carried into the midst of the sea." Ps. 46:2.
22 "Though I walk in the midst of trouble, thou wilt revive me: thou shalt stretch forth thine hand against the wrath of mine enemies, and thy right hand shall save me." Ps. 138:7.
23 "Deliver me from mine enemies, O my God: defend me from them that rise up against me." Ps. 59:1.
24 "For the oppression of the poor, for the sighing of the needy, now will I arise, saith the Lord; I will set *him* in safety *from him that* puffeth at him." Ps. 12:5.
25 Ps. 34:19.
26 "But let all those that put their trust in thee rejoice: let them ever shout for joy, because thou defendest them: let them also that love thy name be joyful in thee." Ps. 5:11.
27 Ps. 118:24.
28 "Rejoice evermore. Pray without ceasing. In every thing give thanks: for this is the will of God in Christ Jesus concerning you." 1 Thes. 5:16–18.

8 A Place of Safety: God is a Refuge
1 Gateway Worship, "The More I Seek You," featuring Melissa Loose, *The First 10 Years Collection*, released 2013.
2 "But let all those that put their trust in thee rejoice: let them ever shout for joy, because thou defendest them: let them also that love thy name be joyful in thee." Ps. 5:11; "But let all those who take refuge *and* put their trust in You rejoice: Let them ever sing *and* shout for joy, Because You make a covering over them *and* defend them; let those also who love Your name be joyful in You *and* be in high spirits." (AMP).
3 "O Lord my God, in thee do I put my trust: save me from all them that persecute me, and deliver me." Ps. 7:1; "O Lord my God, in You I take refuge *and* put my trust; save me from all those who pursue *and* persecute me, and deliver me." (AMP).
4 "Trust in him at all times; ye people, pour out your heart before him: God is a refuge for us. Selah." Ps. 62:8.
5 "But I will sing of thy power; yea, I will sing aloud of thy mercy in the morning: for thou

hast been my defence and refuge in the day of my trouble." Ps. 59:16. David wrote this after discovering Saul was seeking to kill David and he fled.

6   Exod. 33:19–23 (NIV).
7   Exod. 33:21 (NIV).
8   Francis J. Crosby, "He Hideth My Soul," Timeless Truths, accessed May 24, 2021, https://library.timelesstruths.org/music/He_Hideth_My_Soul/.
9   "And I will take away mine hand, and thou shalt see my back parts: but my face shall not be seen." Exod. 33:23.
10 "And when he had removed him, he raised up unto them David to be their king; to whom also he gave testimony, and said, I have found David the *son* of Jesse, as man after mine own heart, which shall fulfil all my will." Acts 13:22.
11 "In God *is* my salvation and my glory: the rock of my strength, *and* my refuge, *is* in God. Trust in him at all times; ye people, pour out your heart before him: God *is* a refuge for us. Selah." Ps. 62:7–8.
12 "I will call on the Lord, *who is* worthy to be praised: so shall I be saved from mine enemies." 2 Sam. 22:4.
13 "Because he hath inclined his ear unto me, therefore will I call upon *him* as long as I live." Psalm 116:2.
14 "And Adam knew his wife again; and she bare a son, and called his name Seth; For God, *said she*, hath appointed me another seed instead of Abel, whom Cain slew. And to Seth, to him also there was born a son; and he called his name Enos: then began men to call upon the name of the Lord." Gen. 4:25–26.
15 "I will call on the Lord, *who is* worthy to be praised: so shall I be saved from mine enemies." 2 Sam. 22:4; "And there he built an altar unto the Lord, and called upon the name of the Lord." Gen. 12:8; "Give thanks unto the Lord, call upon his name, make known his deeds among the people." 1 Chron. 16:8; "O give thanks unto the Lord; call upon his name: make known his deeds among the people." Ps. 105:1; "And call upon me in the day of trouble: I will deliver thee, and thou shalt glorify me." Ps. 50:15; "Be merciful unto me, O Lord: for I cry unto thee daily." Ps. 86:3; "For whosoever shall call upon the name of the Lord shall be saved." Rom. 10:13.
16 Ps. 34:15, 17.
17 "Flee also youthful lusts: but follow righteousness, faith, charity, peace, with them that call on the Lord out of a pure heart." 2 Tim. 2:22.
18 "Have all workers of iniquity no knowledge? who eat up my people *as* they eat bread, and call not upon the Lord." Ps. 14:4; see also Ps. 53:4.
19 "Pour out thy wrath upon the heathen that have not known thee, and upon the kingdoms that have not called upon thy name." Ps. 79:6.
20 "'Refuge' in the Psalms," BibleMesh, accessed May 18, 2021, https://biblemesh.com/

blog/refuge-in-the-psalms/.
21　Ibid.
22　Ibid.
23　"For *it is* not possible that the blood of bulls and of goats should take away sins. [. . .] And every priest standeth daily ministering and offering oftentimes the same sacrifices, which can never take away sin." Heb. 10:4, 11.
24　"But this man [Jesus Christ], after he had offered one sacrifice for sins for ever, sat down on the right hand of God. [. . .] And their sins and iniquities will I remember no more. Now where remission of these *is, there is* no more offering for sin." Heb. 10:12, 17–18.
25　"For sin shall not have dominion over you: for ye are not under the law, but under grace." Rom. 6:14.
26　"Being then made free from sin, ye became the servants of righteousness." Rom. 6:18.
27　"For when ye were the servants of sin, ye were free from righteousness. What fruit had ye then in those things whereof ye are now ashamed? For the end of those things *is* death." Rom. 6:20–21.
28　"But now being made free from sin, and become servants to God, ye have your fruit unto holiness, and the end everlasting life." Rom. 6:22.

9 By the Numbers: We are More Than a Statistic

1　"When thou takest the sum of the children of Israel after their number, then shall they give every man a ransom for his soul unto the Lord, when thou numberest them; that there be no plague among them, when *thou* numberest them. [. . .] And thou shalt take the atonement money of the children of Israel, and shalt appoint it for the service of the tabernacle of the congregation: that it may be a memorial unto the children of Israel before the Lord, to make an atonement for your souls." Ex. 30:12, 16.
2　"And David said to Joab and to the rulers of the people, Go, number Israel from Beer-sheba even to Dan; and bring the number of them to me, that I may know it. [. . .] And Joab gave the sum of the number of the people unto David. And all *they of* Israel were a thousand thousand and an hundred thousand men that drew sword: and Judah *was* four hundred threescore and ten thousand men that drew sword." 1 Chron. 21:2, 5.
3　Mike Aquilina, "How the Bible Reveals the Tensions and Intentions Behind the Census," Angelus, accessed May 18, 2021, https://angelusnews.com/faith/how-the-bible-reveals-the-tensions-and-intentions-behind-the-census/#.
4　Rick Phillips, "Why was David's Census a Great Sin?" Tenth Presbyterian Church, accessed May 18, 2021, https://www.tenth.org/resource-library/articles/why-was-davids-census-a-great-sin/.
5　"Why Did God Discipline David After He Took the Census?" NeverThirsty, accessed May 18, 2021, https://neverthirsty.org/bible-qa/qa-archives/question/why-did-god-dis-

cipline-david-after-he-took-the-census/.
6 "There is neither Jew nor Greek, there is neither bond nor free, there is neither male nor female: for ye are all one in Christ Jesus." Gal. 3:28.
7 U.S. Census Bureau, Current Population Survey, "Living Arrangements of Children under 18 Years/1 and Marital Status of Parents by Age, Sex, Race, and Hispanic Origin/2 and Selected Characteristics of the Child for all Children 2010." table C3, released on the internet November 2010, cited in "The Extent of Fatherlessness," Fathers.com, accessed May 18, 2021, https://fathers.com/statistics-and-research/the-extent-of-fatherlessness/.
8 "The Consequences of Fatherlessness," Fathers.com, accessed May 18, 2021, https://fathers.com/statistics-and-research/the-consequences-of-fatherlessness/.
9 Ibid, citing U.S. Census Bureau, Children's Living Arrangements and Characteristics: March 2011, Table C8. Washington D.C.: 2011.
10 Ibid, citing U.S. Department of Health and Human Services; ASEP Issue Brief: Information on Poverty and Income Statistics. September 12, 2012 http://aspe.hhs.gov/hsp/12/PovertyAndIncomeEst/ib.shtml.
11 Ibid, citing U.S. Department of Health and Human Services. National Center for Health Statistics. Survey on Child Health. Washington, DC, 1993.
12 Ibid, *citing The Lancet, January 25, 2003 • Gunilla Ringbäck Weitoft, MD, Centre for Epidemiology, the National Board of Health and Welfare, Stockholm, Sweden • Irwin Sandler, PhD, professor of psychology and director of the Prevention Research Center, Arizona State University, Tempe • Douglas G. Jacobs, MD, associate clinical professor of psychiatry, Harvard Medical School; and founder and director, The National Depression Screening Program • Madelyn Gould, PhD, MPH, professor of child psychiatry and public health, College of Physicians and Surgeons, Columbia University; and research scientist, New York State Psychiatric Institute.* http://www.webmd.com/baby/news/20030123/absent-parent-doubles-child-suicide-risk.
13 *Psychology Today*, cited in Children's Bureau, "A Father's Impact on Child Development," accessed May 18, 2021, https://www.all4kids.org/news/blog/a-fathers-impact-on-child-development/.
14 Ibid.
15 Ibid.
16 Ibid.
17 Ibid.
18 Ibid.
19 Ibid.
20 "Every year more than 3.6 million referrals are made to child protection agencies involving more than 6.6 million children (a referral can include multiple children)." Child

Help, "Child Abuse Statistics & Facts," accessed May 18, 2021, https://www.childhelp.org/child-abuse-statistics/.

21 "About one in 10 children will be sexually abused before their 18th birthday." Catherine Townsend & Alyssa A. Rheingold, "Estimating a Child Sexual Abuse Prevalence Rate for Practitioners: A Review of Child Sexual Abuse Prevalence Studies," retrieved from www.D2L.org, (Charleston, S.C.: Darkness to Light, 2013), cited in "Child Sexual Abuse Statistics: The Magnitude of the Problem," Darkness to Light, accessed Mar. 18, 2021, www.d2l.org/wp-content/uploads/2017/01/Statistics_1_Magnitude.pdf.

22 Child Help, "Child Abuse Statistics."

23 "Child Sexual Abuse Statistics," Darkness to Light, citing J. J. Broman-Fulks et al., "Sexual assault disclosure in relation to adolescent mental health: Results from the National Survey of Adolescents," *Journal of Clinical Child and Adolescent Psychology*, 36 (2007): 260–266; D. G. Kilpatrick et al., "Violence and risk of PTSD, major depression, substance abuse/dependence, and comorbidity: Results from the National Survey of Adolescents," *Journal of Consulting and Clinical Psychology*, 71 (2003): 692–700; D. Finkelhor et al., "Child and youth victimization known to school, police, and medical officials in a national sample of children and youth," Juvenile Justice Bulletin, no. NCJ 235394, (Washington, DC: United States Department of Justice, Office of Juvenile Justice and Delinquency Prevention); B. E. Saunders et al., "Prevalence, case characteristics, and long-term psychological correlates of child rape among women: A national survey," *Child Maltreatment*, 4 (1999): 187–200; J. Grayson, "Maltreatment and its effects on early brain development," *Virginia Child Protection Newsletter*, 77 (2006): 1–16; R. Leeb, T. Lewis, and A. J. Zolotor, "A review of physical and mental health consequences of child abuse and neglect and implications for practice," *American Journal of Lifestyle Medicine*, 5, no. 5 (2011): 454–468; W. N. Friedrich et al., "Child Sexual Behavior Inventory: Normative, psychiatric, and sexual abuse comparisons," *Child Maltreatment* (2001): 6, 37–49; S. V. McLeer et al., "Psychopathology in non-clinically referred sexually abused children," *Journal of the American Academy of Child and Adolescent Psychiatry*, 37 (1998): 1326–1333; J. G. Noll, C. E. Shenk, and K. T. Putnam, "Childhood sexual abuse and adolescent pregnancy: A meta-analytic update," *Journal of Pediatric Psychology*, 34 (2009): 366–378; E. Olafson, "Child sexual abuse: Demography, impact, and interventions," *Journal of Child & Adolescent Trauma*, 4, no. 1 (2011): 8–21; V. L. Banyard, L. M. Williams, and J. A. Siegel, "The long-term mental health consequences of child sexual abuse: An exploratory study of the impact of multiple traumas in a sample of women," *Journal of Traumatic Stress*, 14 (2001): 697–715; P. Lanier et al., "Child maltreatment and pediatric health outcomes: A longitudinal study of low-income children," *Journal of Pediatric Psychology*, 35, no. 5 (2010): 511–522; E. S. Mullers and M. Dowling, "Mental health consequences of child sexual abuse," *British*

Journal of Nursing, 17, no. 22 (2008): 1428–1433; M. D. De Bellis, E. G. Spratt, and S. R. Hooper, 2011). "Neurodevelopmental biology associated with childhood sexual abuse," *Journal of Child Sexual Abuse*, 20, no. 5 (2011): 548–587; E. Cohen, B. Groves, and K. Kracke, "Understanding children's exposure to violence," *The Safe Start Center Series on Children Exposed to Violence*, 1 (2009): 1–8; J. Tebbutt et al., "Five years after child sexual abuse: Persisting dysfunction and problems of prediction," *Journal of the American Academy of Child & Adolescent Psychiatry*, 36 (1997): 330–339.

24 "Child Sexual Abuse Statistics," Darkness to Light, citing B. E. Saunders et al., "Prevalence, case characteristics, and long-term psychological correlates of child rape among women: A national survey," *Child Maltreatment*, 4 (1999): 187–200; V. L. Banyard, L. M. Williams, and J. A. Siegel, "The long-term mental health consequences of child sexual abuse: An exploratory study of the impact of multiple traumas in a sample of women," *Journal of Traumatic Stress*, 14 (2001): 697–715; B. E. Molnar, S. L. Buka, and R. C. Kessler, "Child sexual abuse and subsequent psychopathology: Results from the National Comorbidity Survey," *American Journal of Public Health*, 91 (2001): 753–760; M. A. Polusny and V. M. Follette, "Long-term correlates of child sexual abuse: theory and review of the empirical literature," *Applied and Preventive Psychology*, 4 (1995): 143–166; M. S. Young et al., "The relationship between childhood sexual abuse and adult mental health among undergraduates: Victim gender doesn't matter," *Journal of Interpersonal Violence*, 22 (2007): 13159–1331.

25 Eph. 3:20.

26 "But the Lord said unto Samuel, Look not on his countenance, or on the height of his stature; because I have refused him: for *the Lord seeth* not as man seeth; for man looketh on the outward appearance, but the Lord looketh on the heart." 1 Sam. 16:7.

27 "O Lord, thou hast searched me, and known *me*. Thou knowest my downsitting and mine uprising, thou understandest my thought afar off. Thou compassest my path and my lyng down, and art acquainted *with* all my ways. For *there is* not a word in my tongue, *but*, lo, O Lord, thou knowest it altogether. Thou hast beset me behind and before, and laid thine hand upon me. *Such* knowledge *is* too wonderful for me; it is high, I cannot *attain* unto It." Psalms 139:1–6.

28 "I will praise thee; for I am fearfully *and* wonderfully made: marvellous *are* thy works; and *that* my soul knoweth right well." Ps. 139:14.

29 "The literal translation of this—as near as can be given—would be, 'I am distinguished by fearful things;' that is, by things in my creation which are suited to inspire awe. I am distinguished among thy works by things which tend to exalt my ideas of God, and to fill my soul with reverent and devout feelings. [. . .] He was made different from inanimate objects, and from the brute creation; he was 'so' made, in the entire structure of his frame, as to fill the mind with wonder." *Barnes' Notes on the Bible*, quoted in "Psalm

30. "For we are his workmanship, created in Christ Jesus unto good works, which God hath before ordained that we should walk in them." Eph. 2:10.
31. "According as he hath chosen us in him before the foundation of the world, that we should be holy and without blame before him in love." Eph. 1:4.
32. "The Lord thy God in the midst of thee *is* mighty; he will save, he will rejoice over thee with joy; he will rest in his love, he will joy over thee with singing." Zeph. 3:17.
33. Zeph. 3:17 (AMP; brackets in the original).
34. "Therefore if any man *be* in Christ, *he is* a new creature: old things are passed away; behold, all things are become new. And all things *are* of God, who hath reconciled us to himself by Jesus Christ, and hath given to us the ministry of reconciliation; To wit, that God was in Christ, reconciling the world unto himself, not imputing their trespasses unto them; and hath committed unto us the word of reconciliation." 2 Cor. 5:17–19.
35. "Behold, what manner of love the Father hath bestowed upon us, that we should be called the sons of God: therefore the world knoweth us not, because it knew him not." 1 John 3:1.
36. "But as many as received him, to them gave he power to become the sons of God, *even* to them that believe on his name: Which were born, not of blood, nor of the will of the flesh, nor of the will of man, but of God." John 1:12–13.
37. "[O] brethren beloved by God, we recognize *and* know that He has selected (chosen) you." 1 Thess. 1:4 (AMP; brackets in the original).
38. "No man can come to me, except the Father which hath sent me draw him: and I will raise him up at the last day." John 6:44.
39. "And you, being dead in your sins and the uncircumcision of your flesh, hath he quickened together with him, having forgiven you all trespasses." Col. 2:13; "If we confess our sins, he is faithful and just to forgive us *our* sins, and to cleanse us from all unrighteousness." 1 John 1:9.
40. "*There is* therefore now no condemnation to them which are in Christ Jesus, who walk not after the flesh, but after the Spirit." Rom. 8:1.
41. "Thus saith the Lord, The heaven *is* my throne, and the earth *is* my footstool." Isa. 66:1; "Nor by the earth; for it is his footstool." Matt. 5:35.
42. "I know both how to be abased, and I know how to abound: every where and in all things I am instructed both to be full and to be hungry, both to abound and to suffer need. I can do all things through Christ which strengtheneth me." Phil. 4:12–13.
43. "That ye may be the children of your Father which is in heaven: for he maketh his sun to rise on the evil and on the good, and sendeth rain on the just and on the unjust." Matt. 5:45.

139:14 Commentaries," Bible Hub, accessed May 19, 2021, https://biblehub.com/commentaries/psalms/139-14.htm.

44 "Who shall separate us from the love of Christ? *shall* tribulation, or distress, or persecution, or famine, or nakedness, or peril, or sword?" Rom. 8:35.
45 Ibid.
46 Rom. 8:37.
47 "Know ye not that ye are the temple of God, and *that* the Spirit of God dwelleth in you?" 1 Cor. 3:16.
48 "But the Comforter, *which is* the Holy Ghost, whom the Father will send in my name, he shall teach you all things, and bring all things to your remembrance, whatsoever I have said unto you." John 14:26.
49 "But as it is written, Eye hath not seen, nor ear heard, neither have entered into the heart of man, the things which God hath prepared for them that love him. But God hath revealed *them* unto us by his Spirit: for the Spirit searcheth all things, yea, the deep things of God. [. . .] Now we have received, not the spirit of the world, but the spirit which is of God; that we might know the things that are freely given to us of God." 1 Cor. 2:9–10, 12.
50 "Ye also, as lively stones, are built up a spiritual house, an holy priesthood, to offer up spiritual sacrifices, acceptable to God by Jesus Christ. [. . .] But ye *are* a chosen generation, a royal priesthood, an holy nation, a peculiar people; that ye should show forth the praises of him who hath called you out of darkness into his marvellous light." 1 Pet. 2:5, 9.
51 "What Does 1 Peter 2:9 Mean?" Knowing-Jesus.com, accessed May 19, 2021, https://dailyverse.knowing-jesus.com/1-peter-2-9.
52 "Let us therefore come boldly unto the throne of grace, that we may obtain mercy, and find grace to help in time of need." Heb. 4:16.

10 Self-Image: What Do You See in the Mirror?

1 "Fostering a Positive Self-Image," Cleveland Clinic, accessed May 19, 2021, https://my.clevelandclinic.org/health/articles/12942-fostering-a-positive-self-image.
2 "Jesus Christ the same yesterday, and today, and for ever." Heb. 13:8.
3 "Fostering a Positive Self-Image," Cleveland Clinic, accessed May 19, 2021, https://my.clevelandclinic.org/health/articles/12942-fostering-a-positive-self-image.
4 Ibid.
5 The Mountain State Centers for Independent Living, quoted in Courtney Ackerman, "What is Self-Image and How Do We Improve It? Definition + Quotes," PositivePsychology.com, accessed May 19, 2021, https://positivepsychology.com/self-image/.
6 My.clevelandclinic.org, "Fostering a Positive Self-Image."
7 PositivePsychology.com, "What is Self-Image?"
8 My.clevelandclinic.org, "Fostering a Positive Self-Image."

9   Ibid.
10 "Jesus Christ the same yesterday, and today, and for ever." Heb. 13:8.
11 "Thus saith the Lord, Let not the wise *man* glory in his wisdom, neither let the mighty *man* glory in his might, let not the rich *man* glory in his riches." Jer. 9:23.
12 "But let him that glorieth glory in this, that he understandeth and knoweth me, that I *am* the Lord which exercise lovingkindness, judgment, and righteousness, in the earth: for in these *things* I delight, saith the Lord." Jer. 9: 24.
13 "For though I would desire to glory, I shall not be a fool; for I will say the truth: but *now* I forbear, lest any man should think of me above that which he seeth me *to be*, or *that* he heareth of me." 2 Cor. 12:6.
14 "Therefore, I take pleasure in infirmities, in reproaches, in necessities, in persecutions, in distresses for Christ's sake: for when I am weak, then am I strong." 2 Cor. 12:10.
15 2 Cor. 12:7.
16 "For this thing I besought the Lord thrice, that it might depart from me." 2 Cor. 12:8.
17 2 Cor. 12:9.
18 Ibid, "Most gladly therefore will I rather glory in my infirmities, that the power of Christ may rest upon me."
19 "Brethren, I count not myself to have apprehended: but *this* one thing *I do*, forgetting those things which are behind, and reaching forth unto those things which are before, I press toward the mark for the prize of the high calling of God in Christ Jesus." Phil. 3:13–14.
20 "[For my determined purpose is] that I may know Him [that I may progressively become more deeply and intimately acquainted with Him, perceiving and recognizing and understanding the wonders of His Person more strongly and more clearly], and that I may in the same way come to know the power outflowing from His resurrection [which it exerts over believers], and that I may so share His sufferings as to be continually transformed [in spirit unto His likeness even] to His death, [in the hope]." Phil. 3:10 (AMP; brackets in the original).
21 Phil. 3:3 (AMP; brackets in the original).
22 "I *am* the Lord thy God, which brought thee out of the land of Egypt: open thy mouth wide, and I will fill it." Ps. 81:10.
23 1 Sam. 16:7.
24 "But we all, with open face beholding as in a glass the glory of the Lord, are changed into the same image from glory to glory, *even* as by the Spirit of the Lord." 2 Cor. 3:18.
25 Mark Shultz, "Father's Eyes," *Come Alive*, Word Entertainment LLC, A Warner/Curb Company, released 2009.

11 Acceptance: We Do Not Need to Struggle to Be Part of the Family

1. Dobson, *Bringing Up Girls*, 21.
2. U.S. Census Bureau, quoted in "What is a family," National Council of Family Relations, accessed May 19, 2021, https://.ncfr.org/ncfr-report/past-issues/summer-2014/what-family.
3. Dana A. Costache, "What makes a family? It's not the marriage certificate," Thrive Global, accessed May 19, 2021, https://thriveglobal.com/stories/what-makes-a-family.
4. National Council of Family Relations, "What is a family."
5. Ibid.
6. "What Makes a Family?," National Center for Families Learning (NCFL), accessed May 19, 2021, https://wonderopolis.org/wonder/what-makes-a-family.
7. Costache, "What makes a family?"
8. Costache, "What makes a family?"
9. "Stepfamily Problems," American Academy of Child and Adolescent Psychiatry, accessed May 19, 2021, https://www.aacap.org/aacap/families_and_youth/facts_for_families/fff-guide/stepfamily-problems-027.aspx.
10. Ibid.
11. "Wherefore seeing we also are compassed about with so great a cloud of witnesses, let us lay aside every weight, and the sin which doth so easily beset *us*, and let us run with patience the race that is set before us." Heb. 12:1.
12. "For ye have not received a spirit of bondage again to fear; but ye have received the Spirit of adoption, whereby we cry, Abba, Father. The Spirit itself beareth witness with our spirit, that we are the children of God." Rom. 8:15–16.
13. "Now therefore ye are no more strangers and foreigners, but fellowcitizens with the saints, and of the household of God." Eph. 2:19.
14. "God setteth the solitary in families." Ps. 68:6.
15. "As we have therefore opportunity, let us do good unto all *men* especially unto them who are of the household of faith." Gal. 6:10.
16. "Or one member be honoured, all the members rejoice with it." 1 Cor. 12:26.
17. "And whether one member suffer, all the members suffer with it." 1 Cor. 12:26.
18. Brooke Krebill, *Uncaged: Break Free by Changing Your Inner Story* (2021), 20–21.
19. "Now when Paul and his company loosed from Paphos, they came to Perga in Pamphylia: and John departing from them returned to Jerusalem." Acts 13:13.
20. "And Barnabas determined to take with them John, whose surname was Mark." Acts 15:37.
21. "But Paul thought not good to take him with them, who departed from them from Pamphylia, and went not with them to the work. And the contention was so sharp between them, that they departed asunder one from the other: and so Barnabas took Mark,

and sailed unto Cyrpus." Acts 15:38–39.

22 "Put on therefore, as the elect of God, holy and beloved, bowels of mercies, kindness, humbleness of mind, meekness, longsuffering; Forbearing *one another*, and forgiving one another, if any man have a quarrel against any: even as Christ forgave you, so also *do ye*." Col. 3:12–13.

23 "Only Luke is with me. Take Mark, and bring him with thee: for he is profitable to me for the ministry." 2 Tim. 4:11.

24 "Have we not power to lead about a sister, a wife, as well as other apostles, and *as* brethren of the Lord, and Cephas? Or I only and Barnabas, have not we power to forbear working?" 1 Cor. 9:5–6.

25 "Rebuke not an elder, but entreat *him* as a father, *and* the younger men as brethren; The elder women as mothers; the younger as sisters, with all purity." 1 Tim. 5:1–2.

26 "That the aged men be sober, grave, temperate, sound in faith, in charity, in patience. The aged women likewise, that *they be* in behaviour as becometh holiness, not false accusers, not given to much wine, teachers of good things; That they may teach the young women to be sober, to love their husbands, to love their children, *To be* discreet, chaste, keepers at home, good, obedient to their own husbands, that the word of God be not blasphemed." Titus 2:2–5.

27 "And let us consider one another to provoke unto love and to good works: Not forsaking the assembling of ourselves together [. . .] but exhorting *one another*." Heb. 10:24–25.

12 Identity: He Gives You a Name

1 Myles Munroe, *The Fatherhood Principle: God's Design and Destiny for Every Man*, (New Kensington, Whitaker House, 2008), 81.

2 Rev. 22:13.

3 "Jesus Christ the same yesterday, today, and for ever." Heb. 13: 8.

4 Carry Underwood, "Last Name," *Carnival Ride*, Universal Music Publishing Group; released October 23, 2007, https://www.azlyrics.com/lyrics/carrieunderwood/lastname.html.

5 Alan Jackson, "I Don't Even Know Your Name," *Who I Am*, Arista Records, released January 12, 1994, http://www.azlyrics.com/lyrics/alanjackson/idontevenknowyourname.html.

6 Dirks Bentley, "My Last Name," *Dierks Bentley*, Capitol Nashville, released October 20, 2003, https://en.wikipedia.org/wiki/My_Last_Name.

7 "And Moses said unto God, Behold, *when* I come unto the children of Israel, and shall say unto them, The God of your fathers hath sent me unto you; and they shall say to me, What *is* his name? what shall I say unto them? And God said unto Moses, I AM THAT I AM: and he said, Thus shalt thou say unto the children of Israel, I AM hath sent me

unto you." Exod. 3:13–14.

8. "And Abraham lifted up his eyes, and looked, and behold behind *him* a ram caught in a thicket by his horns: and Abraham went and took the ram, and offered him up for a burnt offering in the stead of his son. And Abraham called the name of that place Jehovah-jireh: as it is said *to* this day In the mount of the Lord it shall be seen." Gen. 22:13–14.

9. "And said, If thou wilt diligently hearken to the voice of the Lord thy God, and wilt do that which is right in his sight, and wilt give ear to his commandments, and keep all his statutes, I will put none of these diseases upon thee, which I have brought upon the Egyptians: for I *am* the Lord that health thee." Exod. 15:26.

10. "And Moses built an altar, and called the name of it Jehovah-nissi." Exod. 17:15.

11. "Speak thou also unto the children of Israel, saying, Verily my sabbaths ye shall keep: for it *is* a sign between me and you throughout your generations; that *ye* may know that I *am* the Lord that doth sanctify you." Exod. 31:13.

12. "Then Gideon built an altar there unto the Lord, and called it Jehovah-shalom: unto this day it *is* yet in Ophrah of the Abi-ezrites." Judg. 6:24.

13. "The Lord *is* my shepherd; I shall not want." Ps. 23:1.

14. "In the year that king Uzziah died I saw also the Lord sitting upon a throne, high and lifted up, and his train filled the temple. Above it stood the seraphims: each one had six wings; with twain he covered his face, and with twain he covered his feet, and with twain he did fly. And one cried unto another, and said, Holy, holy, holy, *is* the Lord of hosts: the whole earth *is* full of his glory." Isa. 6:1–3.

15. "In his days Judah shall be saved, and Israel shall dwell safely: and this *is* his name whereby he shall be called, 'THE LORD OUR RIGHTEOUSNESS.'" Jer. 23:6.

16. "Flee out of the midst of Babylon, and deliver every man his soul: be not cut off in her iniquity; for this *is* the time of the Lord's vengeance; he will render unto a recompense." Jer. 51:6.

17. "*It was* round about eighteen thousand *measures*: and the name of the city from *that* day *shall be*, The Lord *is* there." Ezek. 48:35.

18. "Who is the image of the invisible God, the firstborn of every creature." Col. 1:15, quoted in *GodWords* (blog), accessed May 20, 2021, http://godwords.org/516/what-does-jesus-mean/.

19. "Wherefore God also hath highly exalted him, and given him a name which is above every name." Phil. 2:9.

20. "That at the name of Jesus every knee should bow, of *things* in heaven, and *things* in earth, and *things* under the earth; And *that* every tongue should confess that Jesus Christ *is* Lord, to the glory of God the Father." Phil. 2:10–11.

21. Acts 4:12.

22. "Go ye therefore, and teach all nations, baptizing them in the name of the Father, and of the Son, and of the Holy Ghost." Matt. 28:19.
23. "Then Peter said unto them, Repent, and be baptized every one of you in the name of Jesus Christ for the remission of sins, and ye shall receive the gift of the Holy Ghost." Acts 2:38.
24. "Go ye therefore, and teach all nations, baptizing them in the name of the Father, and of the Son, and of the Holy Ghost." Matt. 28:19; "Thus it is written, and thus it behooved Christ to suffer, and to rise from the dead the third day: And that repentance and remission of sins should be preached in his name among all nations, beginning at Jerusalem." Luke 24:46–47.
25. "Then Peter said unto them, Repent, and be baptized every one of you in the name of Jesus Christ for the remissions of sins, and ye shall receive the gift of the Holy Ghost. For the promise is unto you, and to your children, and to all that are afar off, *even* as many as the Lord our God shall call. And with many other words did he testify and exhort, saying, Save yourselves from this untoward generation. Then they that gladly received his word were baptized: and the same day there were added *unto them* about three thousand souls." Acts 2:38–41; "But when they believed Philip preaching the things concerning the kingdom of God, and the name of Jesus Christ, they were baptized, both men and women." Acts 8:12; "For as yet he was fallen upon none of them: only they were baptized in the name of the Lord Jesus." Acts 8:16; "Can any man forbid water, that these should not be baptized, which have received the Holy Ghost as well as we? And he commanded them to be baptized in the name of the Lord. Then prayed they him to tarry certain days." Acts 10:47–48; "And he said unto them, Unto what then were ye baptized? And they said, Unto John's baptism. Then said Paul, John verily baptized with the baptism of repentance, saying unto the people, that they should believe on him which should come after him, that is, on Christ Jesus. When they heard *this*, they were baptized in the name of the Lord Jesus." Acts 19:3–5,
26. "In the beginning was the Word, and the Word was with God, and the Word was God. [. . .] And the Word was made flesh, and dwelt among us, (and we beheld his glory, the glory as of the only begotten of the Father,) full of grace and truth." John 1:1, 14.
27. "For as many of you as have been baptized into Christ have put on Christ." Gal. 3:27.

13 God's Transforming Love: Turning Regrets into Thanksgiving
1. "Regret," GoodTherapy, accessed May 20, 2021, https://www.goodtherapy.org/blog/psychpedia/regret.
2. Ibid.
3. Ibid.
4. "Then took they him, and led *him*, and brought him into the high priest's house. And

Peter followed afar off." Luke 22:54.

5. "And when they had kindled a fire in the midst of the hall, and were set down together, Peter sat down among them. But a certain maid beheld him as he sat by the fire, and earnestly looked upon him, and said, This man was also with him. And he denied him, saying, Woman, I know him not. And after a little while another saw him, and said, Thou art also of them. And Peter said, Man, I am not. And about the space of one hour after another confidently affirmed, saying, Of a truth this *fellow* also was with him: for he is a Galilaean. And Peter said, Man, I know not what thou sayest. And immediately, while he yet spake, the cock crew. And the Lord turned, and looked upon Peter. And Peter remembered the word of the Lord, how he had said unto him, Before the cock crow, thou shalt deny me thrice." Luke 22:55–61.

6. "And the Lord turned, and looked upon Peter, And Peter remembered the word of the Lord, how he had said unto him, Before the cock crow, thou shalt deny me thrice. And Peter went out, and wept bitterly." Luke 22:61–62.

7. "After these things Jesus showed himself again to the disciples at the sea of Tiberias; and on this wise showed he *himself*." John 21:1.

8. "So when they had dined, Jesus saith to Simon Peter, Simon, *son* of Jonas, lovest thou me more than these? He saith unto him, Yea, Lord; thou knowest that I love thee. He saith unto him, Feed my lambs. He saith to him again the second time, Simon, *son* of Jonas, lovest thou me? He saith unto him, Yea, Lord; thou knowest that I love thee. He saith unto him, Feed my sheep. He saith unto him the third time, Simon, *son* of Jonas, lovest thou me? Peter was grieved because he said unto him the third time, Lovest thou me? And he said unto him, Lord, thou knowest all things: thou knowest that I love thee. Jesus saith *unto* him, Feed my sheep." John 21:15–17.

9. "So when they had dined, Jesus saith to Simon Peter, Simon, *son* of Jonas, lovest thou me more than these? He saith unto him, Yea, Lord; thou knowest that I love thee. He saith unto him, Feed my lambs. He saith to him again the second time, Simon, *son* of Jonas, lovest thou me? He saith unto him, Yea, Lord; thou knowest that I love thee. He saith unto him, Feed my sheep. He saith unto him the third time, Simon, *son* of Jonas, lovest thou me? Peter was grieved because he said unto him the third time, Lovest thou me? And he said unto him, Lord, thou knowest all things; thou knowest that I love thee. Jesus saith *unto* him, Feed my sheep." John 21:15–17.

10. "Restore unto me the joy of thy salvation; and uphold me *with thy* free spirit." Ps. 51:12.

11. "And it came to pass, when Joseph was come unto his brethren, that they stripped Joseph out of his coat, *his* coat of *many* colours that *was* on him; And they took him, and cast him into a pit: and the pit *was* empty, *there* was no water in it. And they sat down to eat bread: and they lifted up their eyes and looked, and, behold, a company of Ishmeelites came from Gilead with their camels bearing spicery and balm and myrrh, going

to carry *it* down to Egypt. And Judah said unto his brethren, What profit *is it* if we slay our brother, and conceal his blood? Come, and let us sell him to the Ishmeelites, and let not our hand be upon him; for he *is* our brother *and* our flesh. And his brethren were content. Then there passed by Midianites merchantmen; and they drew and lifted up Joseph out of the pit, and sold Joseph to the Ishmeelites for twenty *pieces* of silver: and they brought Joseph into Egypt." Gen. 37:23–28.

12 "And it came to pass about this time, that *Joseph* went into the house to do his business; and *there was* none of the men of the house there within. And she caught him by his garment, saying, Lie with me: and he left his garment in her hand, and fled, and got him out. And it came to pass, when she saw that he had left his garment in her hand, and was fled forth, That she called unto the men of her house, and spake unto them, saying, See, he hath brought in an Hebrew unto us to mock us; he came in unto me to lie with me, and I cried with a loud voice: And it came to pass, when he heard that I lifted up my voice and cried, that he left his garment with me, and fled, and got him out. And she laid up his garment by her, until his lord came home. And she spake unto him according to these words, saying, The Hebrew servant, which thou hast brought unto us, came in unto me to mock me: And it came to pass, as I lifted up my voice and cried, that he left his garment with me, and fled out. And it came to pass, when his master heard the words of his wife, which she spake unto him, saying, After this manner did thy servant to me; that his wrath was kindled. And Joseph's master took him, and put him into the prison, a place where the king's prisoners *were* bound: and he was there in the prison." Gen. 39:11–20.

13 "And the thing was good in the eyes of Pharaoh, and in the eyes of all his servants. And Pharaoh said unto his servants, Can we find *such a one as* this *is*, a man in whom the spirit of God *is*? And Pharaoh said unto Joseph, Forasmuch as God hath shown thee all this, *there is* none so discreet and wise as thou *art*: Thou shalt be over my house, and according unto thy word shall all my people be ruled: only in the throne will I be greater than thou. And Pharaoh said unto Joseph, See, I have set thee over all the land of Egypt. And Pharaoh took off his ring from his hand, and put it upon Joseph's hand, and arrayed him in vestures of fine linen, and put a gold chain about his neck; And he made him to ride in the second chariot which he had; and they cried before him, Bow the knee: and he made him *ruler* over all the land of Egypt." Gen. 41:37–43.

14 "And Joseph's ten brethren went down to buy corn in Egypt." Gen. 42:3.

15 "And he turned himself about from them, and wept." Gen. 42:24; "And Joseph made haste; for his bowels did yearn upon his brother: and he sought *where* to weep; and he entered into *his* chamber, and wept there." Gen. 43:30.

16 Gen. 50:19–20.

17 Rom. 8:28.

18 "Let all bitterness, and wrath, and anger, and clamour, and evil speaking, be put away from you, with all malice." Eph. 4:31.
19 "Search me, O God, and know my heart: try me, and know my thoughts: And see if *there be* any wicked way in me, and lead me in the way everlasting." Ps. 139:23–24.
20 Phil 4:6–7.
21 Phil. 3:13.
22 Helen Howarth Lemmel, "Turn Your Eyes Upon Jesus," Hymnary.org, accessed May 24, 2021, https://hymnary.org/text/o_soul_are_you_weary_and_troubled.
23 Rom. 15:13.

www.ingramcontent.com/pod-product-compliance
Lightning Source LLC
Chambersburg PA
CBHW030905080526
44589CB00010B/155